# before we begin

Themed prayers leading into worship

## Nick Fawcett

kevin
**mayhew**

First published in 2004 by

KEVIN MAYHEW LTD
Buxhall, Stowmarket, Suffolk, IP14 3BW
E-mail: info@kevinmayhewltd.com

9 8 7 6 5 4 3 2 1 0

ISBN  1 84417 333 X
Catalogue No  1500755

Cover design by Angela Selfe
Edited and typeset by Katherine Laidler
Printed in Great Britain

# Contents

# Introduction

It's Sunday and just a few minutes before the service. A hush descends in the vestry, those gathered there looking round, waiting for someone to give a lead. What happens next varies from church to church, tradition to tradition. In some places, prayer is offered by the officiating minister; in others it may be open to all present, anyone being free to offer extemporary prayer. Each approach has its strengths and weaknesses. Formal patterns can seem dry, almost perfunctory, especially if the same prayer is used week after week or if prayers offered are phrased in florid archaic language. Informal patterns, by contrast, may carry a far greater sense of being offered from the heart, yet do little if anything to set the scene for worship, still less tie in with the theme or mood of the service to follow.

There is, of course, no right or wrong way to pray before worship. I have personally valued occasions when individuals have asked God to give me strength, guidance and wisdom in leading a service. On the other hand, I can recall times of prayer in the vestry that have gone on almost longer than the service itself! Perhaps the prayers I have found most meaningful have been those that tied in with the theme or occasion to be celebrated; those, in other words, directly related to the worship they introduced.

My aim in writing this book has been to offer a resource with that goal in mind. A variety of prayers are offered, thematically arranged and each written in everyday language, together with additional prayers for special days and events such as Christmas, Holy Week, Easter, Mothering Sunday, Father's Day, Harvest Festival and Remembrance Day. Each prayer is linked, though not rigidly tied, to a specific Bible reading, usually from the gospels but occasionally from elsewhere in the New Testament.

Whatever the custom within your church, it is my hope that something within these pages may prove of value, able to focus people's thoughts upon God so that they are better prepared to hear his word, glimpse his presence, and offer their response with body, mind and soul.

NICK FAWCETT

# Advent

## 1
### *Matthew 24:36-44*

Lord Jesus Christ,
> we come today yearning to welcome, worship, meet and greet you,
> but conscious also that,
> just as many were not ready to receive you
> when first you entered our world,
> so we too can be less prepared than we think,
> our narrow expectations or misplaced assumptions
> closing our minds to your presence among us.

So we ask that, as we draw near to you,
> you will draw near to us,
> stirring our hearts and capturing our imagination.

Prepare us to recognise you afresh at work in our lives and our world,
> and so make us ready to serve you,
> today and always.

Amen.

## 2
### *Matthew 25:1-13*

Lord Jesus Christ,
> prepare our hearts to meet you in this time of worship
> and when you return in glory to establish your kingdom.

Confront, instruct and enable us by your Spirit,
> so that we will be awake and alert,
> equipped to live each moment
> as though the day of your coming has dawned,
> and ready to welcome you whenever it might be.

Amen.

# 3
## *Matthew 11:2-11*

Lord,
    as you spoke through John the Baptist,
    and through the prophets before him,
    speak now through this time of worship,
    and through all who will share in leading it.
Behind the voices we hear,
    the words we read and the message we listen to
    may we hear your voice,
    calling, confronting,
    leading, loving,
    enthusing and enabling.
Open our ears, our minds and our souls
    to your word of truth,
    the Word made flesh,
    Jesus Christ our Lord.
Amen.

# 4
## *John 1:29-42*

Gracious God,
    help us, like John the Baptist before us
    and so many others who have followed in his footsteps,
    to see the light of Christ and bear witness to it,
    pointing through word and deed to his love for all.
Open our lives, through your Spirit, to his presence among us now,
    and help us to live in such a way that his light may shine in us
    and through us,
    bringing glory to you.
Amen.

## 5
### *Matthew 3:1-12*

Father God,
   just as you sent your servant John into the wilderness
   to prepare the way of the Lord
   and make ready your people to receive him,
   so prepare us now to respond afresh to the gift of Christ
   and to all that you offer us through him.
Give us a readiness truly to listen, learn, worship and respond,
   receiving the forgiveness he extends
   and the renewal he makes possible,
   and giving back in return our heartfelt gratitude
   expressed in true commitment and faithful service.
In his name we pray.
Amen.

## 6
### *John 1:6-8, 19-28*

Sovereign God,
   we are reminded today of how,
   through the prophets and the testimony of John the Baptist,
   you brought challenge as well as promise,
   a message that disturbed as much as it delighted,
   that unsettled as much as uplifted.
Help us now as we worship,
   and each day as we strive to follow Jesus,
   to be open to your voice in the wilderness,
   your word that probes deep within,
   searching the thoughts of the heart
   and confronting us with the challenge of the gospel.
However demanding it may be,
   teach us to hear,
   to listen
   and to respond,
   through Jesus Christ our Lord.
Amen.

## 7
### *Luke 1:39-55*

Gracious God,
reminded at this season of your awesome gift in Christ,
we want to respond,
to offer something in return as a sign of our gratitude
for all you have done and continue to do.
We would bring you our worship –
not just well-intentioned thoughts and words
but our wholehearted adoration and joyful thanksgiving.
We would bring you our lives –
not just token deeds or outward show,
but hearts consecrated to your service,
embodying your love for all,
your care and compassion for everything you have made.
Receive, then, this time set aside for you
as a small yet sincere way of acknowledging your goodness,
and through it equip us to live as your people
this and every day.
Amen.

## 8
### *Luke 3:7-18*

Eternal God,
we celebrate today the fulfilment of your promises of old
through the coming of the Messiah,
foretold by the prophets and long yearned for –
a Saviour to deliver your people and establish your kingdom,
bringing freedom, life and new beginnings.
We celebrate how wonderfully you honoured those promises
in Christ,
granting through him more than we can ever ask or imagine.
Help us now, as we worship you, to celebrate your faithfulness
and to trust you completely for the future,
knowing that we can depend on you, come what may,
certain that what you have pledged will be accomplished
and that nothing can ever separate us from your love
in Jesus Christ our Lord.
Amen.

# 9

## *Mark 1:1-8*

Redeemer God,
    as we prepare to celebrate the birth of your Son,
    speak through all we share together now:
    the singing of hymns,
    the reading of Scripture,
    the preaching of your word,
    the offering of prayers –
    these and so much more.
Break through all that separates us from you and him:
    over-familiarity,
    indifference,
    self-will,
    disobedience,
    narrowness of vision,
    weakness of resolve.
Move among us through your Spirit –
    inspiring,
    instructing,
    revealing,
    renewing –
    so that we may be equipped now to worship
    and always to serve.
Amen.

# 10

## *Luke 1:26-38*

Almighty God,
    we recall at this joyful season how,
    through her willingness to hear your word
    and commit herself to your service,
    you were able to use Mary to fulfil your purpose,
    entering our world,
    inaugurating your kingdom
    and bringing closer that day when sorrow and suffering,
    darkness and death
    will be no more.

Help us, then, as we gather now to worship,
   to hear your word
   and to respond with similar obedience,
   prepared to be used as you see fit.
Through our discipleship,
   weak and feeble though it might be,
   may your grace be revealed,
   your love made known
   and your world enriched.
Amen.

# 11

## *Matthew 1:18-25*

Lord Jesus Christ,
   born to Mary,
   coming to our world through her,
   be born afresh in us
   that we might be born again through you.
Touch now this time of worship
   that the message of your birth,
   so familiar and well loved,
   will speak afresh with new power and clarity,
   thrilling our hearts
   and filling us with joy and gratitude.
Draw close to us now,
   that through welcoming you into our lives
   and opening ourselves once more to your renewing power
   you may reach out through us to the world,
   bringing hope and healing,
   light and life,
   to the glory of your name.
Amen.

# _____ Adversity, faith in times of _____

## 12

### _Mark 4:35-41_

Lord Jesus Christ,
  fasten our thoughts on you,
  fashion our lives
  and deepen our faith,
  so that, trusting you more completely,
  we will be equipped to withstand times of testing and challenge –
  able to ride out the storms of trouble and tragedy,
  sickness and suffering,
  knowing that, even there, you are with us,
  speaking your word of peace and bidding the waves to die down.
May we find in you stillness of mind and tranquillity of spirit,
  now and for evermore.
Amen.

## 13

### _Luke 8:22-25_

Living God,
  we come in faith to worship you,
  yet we come also conscious that our faith is so very weak,
  all too easily undermined in the storms of life,
  sinking without trace when trouble and danger threaten.
Forgive us,
  and speak again of your loving purpose and sovereign power.
Teach us that even in times of turmoil you are there,
  nothing finally able to overcome your will,
  and in that confidence may we put our trust
  now and always.
Amen.

## 14

*Matthew 14:22-33*

Lord Jesus Christ,
    speak your word now in the turmoil of our world,
    in the confusion of life,
    and especially in the hearts of those present today
    who find themselves all at sea,
    tossed about in storms of sorrow, suffering, anxiety and despair.
Bring order out of chaos,
    confidence out of fear,
    faith out of doubt
    and peace out of unrest –
    the certain knowledge that nothing,
    not even death itself,
    can finally overwhelm us.
In your name we pray.
Amen.

## 15

*Luke 17:5-10*

Lord of all,
    remind us today that you are a faithful and loving God,
    a God who hears the cry of your people
    and answers them in their distress.
Though you do not guarantee exemption
    from pain, sorrow or hardship,
    teach us that you promise always
    to give us strength to meet adversity,
    the inner presence of your Spirit
    to encourage, comfort, equip and inspire,
    bringing peace even in turmoil
    and laughter even through tears.
Help us, then, to trust you whatever life brings,
    through Jesus Christ our Lord.
Amen.

## 16
### *Luke 8:26-39*

Sovereign God,
   in all the trials and traumas life brings,
   and in our troubled world scarred by tragedy and turmoil,
   remind us that you are with us in bad times as much as any,
   sharing in our sorrow and suffering,
   understanding our fear and anxiety,
   and seeking to strengthen, support, heal and help.
Teach us, then, through this time of worship,
   that though life may test us to the limit,
   bringing much that is hard to bear or to see your hand in,
   nothing finally can separate us from your love,
   your hand leading us not just now
   but for all eternity,
   through Jesus Christ our Lord.
Amen.

## 17
### *Matthew 24:1-14*

Eternal God,
   lead our thoughts today
   and our lives always,
   that we might be equipped to keep faith with you.
Guard us from what might lead us astray,
   strengthen us in times of testing
   and protect us from evil.
Give us strength to follow you to the end –
   through joy or sorrow,
   good or bad,
   pleasure or pain –
   trusting in your saving love and sovereign will,
   until all is accomplished,
   through Jesus Christ our Lord.
Amen.

# Awe and wonder in worship

## 18

### *John 1:1-14*

Sovereign God –
mighty and mysterious,
immortal,
invisible –
as we come together in your presence
we do not simply want to go through the motions of worship,
to do what's expected of us;
we want to see Jesus,
recognising him at work in the world and involved in our lives,
present and active through his Spirit.
Broaden our vision and enlarge our understanding,
that we might glimpse more of his grace and truth,
love and light,
power and glory,
and so catch clearer sight also of you,
our eyes opened to your awesome majesty through him.
Amen.

## 19

### *John 16:12-15*

Sovereign God,
　mighty and mysterious,
　before all,
　within all,
　above all,
　we would more truly honour you,
　more completely know you
　and more faithfully serve you.
Give us today, then,
　a fuller sense of your greatness,
　a deeper awareness of your presence
　and a firmer understanding of your will,
　that we may worship, love and serve you
　in spirit and in truth,　　*In the talks*
　through Jesus Christ our Lord.
Amen.

## 20

### *Ephesians 3:7-21*

Great and wonderful God,
　words fail us in your presence,
　yet we cannot keep silent;
　our minds reel in awe and wonder,
　yet we yearn to know you more;
　your ways are not our ways,
　nor your thoughts our thoughts,
　but our hearts are restless within us
　and our spirits troubled
　until we find our home in you.
Draw near, then, as we worship,
　and, by your grace, enlarge our understanding,
　enrich our faith,
　and enfold us in your love,
　so that knowing you more fully,
　we may serve you more truly,
　through Jesus Christ our Lord.
Amen.

## 21
### *Mark 9:2-9*

Lord Jesus Christ,
    however much we think we know you,
    however clearly we believe we have understood your greatness,
    open our eyes today to a deeper awareness,
    fuller picture
    and yet more wonderful vision of who and what you are.
Teach us that our minds can only begin to grasp your glory,
    at best glimpsing part of the truth,
    for there is always more to be revealed,
    more to learn,
    more to catch our imagination and thrill our souls.
Grant, then, as we worship you,
    that your radiance might burst afresh into our lives,
    so that we might return to the daily routine
    determined to know, love and serve you better,
    to the glory of your name.
Amen.

## 22
### *Matthew 17:1-9*

Lord Jesus Christ,
    as we come to worship, give us a sense of awe and wonder,
    an awareness of the privilege we have in knowing you,
    receiving your Spirit
    and being called your people.
Grant us a glimpse of your glory that brings home to us
    your greatness and goodness,
    care and compassion,
    purpose and pardon –
    a foretaste that fills us with joy
    and causes us to kneel in adoration,
    overcome with amazement, thankfulness and love.

Teach us never to become casual in our devotion,
    blasé, complacent or indifferent,
    but to come rather with reverence and humility,
    eager to offer you, through word and deed,
    the adulation you deserve.
In your name we pray.
Amen.

## 23

### *Luke 9:28-43*

Sovereign God,
    as Peter, James and John caught a glimpse of your radiance
    on the mountaintop,
    revealed in Christ,
    so may we today see your glory more clearly –
    your light shining in our hearts,
    firing our imagination,
    filling us with joy
    and fanning the flames of faith.
Help us, confronted by the mystery and wonder of your presence,
    to recognise that, however much we have understood,
    you have far more to reveal,
    our grasp of your greatness and experience of your love still partial,
    needing always to be open to new horizons.
Speak, then,
    and open our eyes,
    in the name of Christ.
Amen.

# Call of God

## 24

### *Luke 3:15-17, 21-22*

Mighty God,
    challenge us through the example of Jesus –
    his humble acceptance of his calling
    and his faithfulness to the last –
    to consider our own calling:
    to follow as his disciples,
    his witnesses,
    his people.
Instruct, equip and inspire us,
    that, by his grace,
    we might show similar faithfulness and humility,
    and honour the commitment we have made,
    today and every day.
Amen.

## 25

### *Mark 1:4-11*

Lord Jesus Christ,
    we praise you today for your obedience to God's call,
    your willingness to commit yourself
    to the way of service, sacrifice and self-denial
    so that we might become children of God.
Give us, as we worship you,
    a clearer understanding of all that means –
    the joy it offers and responsibility it entails –
    so that we might commit ourselves more fully to you
    and respond in turn to your call,
    for your name's sake.
Amen.

## 26
### *Mark 1:14-20*

Lord Jesus Christ,
  help us today to hear again your call to discipleship,
  and faithfully to follow wherever you would lead.
May the good news of your living, dying and rising among us
  resonate afresh deep within,
  stirring us to sincere repentance,
  deeper faith
  and renewed service.
Teach us now to live more authentically as your people,
  in the light of your kingdom.
Amen.

## 27
### *Matthew 3:13-17*

Lord Jesus Christ,
  Redeemer,
  deliverer,
  we remember today your obedience to God's call –
  your readiness to commit your life
  to the way of service and sacrifice,
  surrendering yourself in order to save others.
Challenge us through that example
  to consider our own faith and calling:
  the nature of our discipleship
  and the priorities we set in our lives.
Help us, remembering all you have done for us
  and celebrating the love you continue so constantly to show,
  to commit ourselves again to the growth of your kingdom
  on earth as it is in heaven.
Amen.

# Christmas

### 28
### *Luke 2:1-7*

Sovereign God,
    with Mary and Joseph gazing into the manger,
    with shepherds hurrying to and from the stable,
    with angels praising you on high,
    with wise men kneeling before the Christ-child,
    and with generations across the years
    who have known and loved your Son,
    experiencing his presence in their lives,
    so now we join to marvel and celebrate,
    offering you our heartfelt worship and joyful praise
    for your gift beyond words,
    Jesus Christ our Lord.
Amen.

### 29
### *Luke 2:8-20*

Sovereign God,
    though we have heard it so many times before,
    and though the words of readings and carols we will share today
    are so familiar we know them almost back to front,
    grant that through the worship we bring you
    our hearts may thrill again to the good news of Christ,
    and our spirits soar at the message of his coming.
Grant us new insights and deeper understanding,
    so that our faith may be enriched and our joy increased
    as we celebrate the great gift of your Son –
    glad tidings yesterday,
    today
    and every day.
Amen.

## 30

### *Luke 2:25-36*

Lord Jesus Christ,
   come among us in this time of worship.
As you came in Bethlehem and will come again in glory,
   so, we ask, draw near now
   and open our eyes to your presence among us here.
Speak your word,
   impart your blessing,
   grant your mercy
   and renew our faith,
   so that we may be ready at every moment to welcome you
   and equipped to live more truly to your praise and glory.
Amen.

## 31

### *John 1:1-14*

Loving God,
   remind us that in taking flesh and being born as a baby,
   you identified yourself fully with humankind,
   not imposing yourself upon us
   but drawing alongside,
   inviting a response.
Remind us that you made yourself vulnerable,
   exposing yourself to persecution and rejection from the beginning,
   willingly bearing the price of love.
Open our hearts today to respond –
   freely, gladly and reverently –
   ready to risk something for you
   who risked so much for us.
Amen.

## 32

### *Luke 2:8-20*

God of love,
    recalling today how shepherds hurried to Bethlehem,
    eager to see for themselves the truth of what they had heard,
    so we too are hungry to meet afresh with Christ,
    to offer him our worship,
    to rejoice in his presence
    and to make our personal response to your coming through him.
Direct, then, our thoughts and actions in this time of worship,
    so that through our hymns, readings, prayers,
    reflection and fellowship
    we may see and know you better,
    appreciating more fully the wonder of this season
    and the good news it proclaims for all.
Amen.

## 33

### *Luke 2:15-21*

Lord Jesus Christ,
    like the shepherds of old
    we come with hearts ablaze to celebrate your birth,
    to kneel in wonder,
    to offer our thanksgiving
    and to respond personally to you.
May we, like them, thrill to the good news of your coming,
    and go on our way rejoicing,
    making known to those we meet
    everything we have found to be true in you.
In your name we pray.
Amen.

## 34
### *Matthew 2:1-12*

Lord Jesus Christ,
    we celebrate today how wise men were prepared to seek,
    and keep on seeking,
    persevering despite setbacks and disappointments
    until they found you.
We remember how you promised that all who seek will find,
    that those who ask will receive,
    that to those who knock the door will be opened,
    and so we come now,
    asking for your guidance and seeking to know you better,
    so that, drawing ever closer to you,
    we may offer our love and our lives in glad response,
    to the glory of your name.
Amen.

## 35
### *Luke 2:22-40*

Living God,
    like Anna and Simeon before us,
    may our hearts leap for joy as we celebrate your coming in Christ,
    the one anticipated for so long
    and on whom the hopes of so many rested.
Help us to recognise in him the fulfilment of your promises
    and answer to our needs;
    the one who brings unsettling challenge yet also offers peace;
    who brings light and life
    not only to us but also to all the world.
Teach us to respond faithfully,
    offering our grateful praise,
    and witnessing in word and deed
    to everything you have done through him.
In his name we pray.
Amen.

# Commitment

*see also* Daily life: serving God in

## 36
### *John 13:31-35*

Lord Jesus Christ,
  we come to you in worship,
  seeking to learn more of you
  and to welcome you more fully into our lives.
We come,
  yearning to love as you have loved us –
  to show the truth of our faith
  and the authenticity of our discipleship
  through our devotion to one another and to you,
  and through our concern for others.
Help us, through this service,
  to recognise the ways in which we fall short of that calling,
  to acknowledge these honestly to you,
  and to open our hearts afresh to your grace,
  so that your love might grow within us
  and overflow to your praise and glory.
Amen.

## 37
### *Luke 14:25-33*

Gracious God,
  help us today to grasp more clearly
  that it is in giving we receive,
  in losing we find,
  in sacrifice we find reward,
  and in dying to self that we rise to new life.

In that knowledge, may we willingly accept the cost of discipleship,
    knowing that, whatever is asked of us,
    the rewards of your kingdom are beyond price.
Open our eyes afresh today to that truth,
    through Jesus Christ our Lord.
Amen.

## 38

### Mark 7:1-8

Almighty God,
    help us truly to worship you –
    to offer not superficial show,
    empty piety,
    lifeless ritual
    or outward observance,
    but heartfelt praise,
    true thanksgiving,
    genuine penitence,
    sacrificial commitment,
    meaningful intercession
    and a real hunger and thirst to know and serve you better.
Work within us now,
    so that what we declare with our lips
    we may believe in our hearts
    and display in our lives,
    to your glory.
Amen.

## 39
### *John 14:1-14*

Lord Jesus Christ,
   we believe you to be the way, the truth and the life,
   but our faith is flawed and our commitment weak,
   so that, all too easily and often, we go our own way,
   losing sight of truth
   and denying ourselves the fullness of life you offer.
Guide us now, as we worship,
   so that we might walk with you more closely,
   believe more truly,
   and live more faithfully,
   to the glory of God the Father.
Amen.

## 40
### *Matthew 16:21-28*

Lord Jesus Christ,
   we want to honour you by living as your disciples
   and walking in your way,
   but we find it hard,
   our inclinations so very different to your own.
Reveal to us, we pray, more of what it means to follow you,
   more about the true nature of discipleship.
Help us to grasp the meaning of your kingdom,
   where losers are winners,
   the first are last,
   and those who lose their life for your sake will truly find it.
Teach us now,
   by your grace.
Amen.

## 41

### *Luke 12:32-40*

Sovereign God,
  teach us to use the time, gifts, health and opportunities you give us
  wisely,
  creatively
  and fruitfully.
Remind us here today of what you ask of us,
  what you expect from us –
  the responsibilities involved in Christian discipleship –
  and, by your grace,
  help us not to be found wanting.
In Christ's name we pray.
Amen.

## 42

### *Luke 12:49-56*

Living God,
  reveal to us more of your will
  and equip us to honour it.
Save us from taking the path of least resistance,
  opting for peace where there is no peace
  or pretending all is well when the reality is otherwise.
Give us instead the faith and courage we need
  to stand up for what is right,
  even if that risks alienating people,
  including, perhaps, those we love.
Hear us and help us, O God,
  in the name of Christ.
Amen.

## 43

*Luke 9:51-62*

Lord Jesus Christ,
   teach us today to put you first in our lives,
   seeking to honour and serve you not as an afterthought,
   an optional extra,
   or as an occasional pursuit,
   but wholeheartedly,
   genuinely committed to you with body, mind and spirit.
May our response to you shape everything we do,
   rather than everything we do put time for you on hold.
Call us afresh now
   and help us truly to be your people,
   by your grace.
Amen.

# Daily life, glimpsing God in

*see also* Time and space for God

## 44

### *Matthew 6:25-34*

Living God,
    teach us, through spending time with you now,
    to spend time with you always;
    through hearing your voice in this time and place set apart,
    to hear you equally in the daily routine of life.
Help us to see around us,
    in the flowers of the field and birds of the air,
    signs of your care, love and gracious provision,
    and so may we trust you better,
    focusing on the things in life that matter –
    your kingdom and righteousness –
    and leaving all else in your hands.
Teach us to take every day as it comes,
    not brooding or fretting about the future,
    but celebrating each moment you give us
    and living it to the full,
    confident that you know all our needs and will not fail us.
Amen.

## 45
### *Mark 10:46-52*

Lord Jesus Christ,
  as we gather to worship you,
  help us to see you here among us,
  so that we might equally see you everywhere.
Give us a clearer picture of your greatness and power,
  your love and mercy,
  your purpose for us and for all.
Broaden our vision
  and help us to catch a glimpse of you in all your glory,
  filling us with joy, faith, hope and love,
  now and always.
Amen.

## 46
### *Matthew 18:15-20*

Lord Jesus Christ,
  you promise that where two or three are gathered in your name,
  you will be there in the midst of them,
  and so we come now,
  eager to meet with you:
  to hear your voice,
  receive your guidance,
  offer our worship
  and do your will.
Come among us through your Spirit
  and help us to sense your nearness.
Fill our hearts and minds,
  so that when we return to the daily business of life
  we will know you with us there too
  and be equipped to walk in your way,
  faithful and true to our journey's end.
Amen.

# Daily life, serving God in

### 47
*Luke 6:17-26*

Lord Jesus Christ,
    we want to worship you
    not through fine-sounding words or empty ritual
    but through truly living as your people,
    walking in your way and honouring your will.
Help us to understand what it means
    to be part of your kingdom here on earth;
    to recognise that it turns so many of our aspirations
    and assumptions upside down.
Equip us not only to grasp that truth,
    but also to apply it to daily life,
    so that we might find in you true riches and fulfilment,
    lasting joy and love,
    life able to satisfy not just now but for all eternity.
Amen.

### 48
*Matthew 22:15-22*

Lord of all,
    teach us as citizens of heaven to live also as citizens of earth,
    conducting ourselves in such a way as to bring honour to you.
Show us what it means to be your people in the daily business of life;
    how best we might fulfil our responsibilities and duties to others
    while staying true to you,
    recognising your ultimate sovereignty over all.
Speak to us now,
    and grant us the wisdom, sincerity and faith we need
    to walk as your people,
    within your world.
Amen.

## 49

### *Mark 2:23-3:6*

Living God,
    with generations across the centuries,
    we come on this day set apart for you,
    making space in our lives,
    offering our worship,
    seeking your mercy
    and looking for guidance.
Answer our prayers
    and respond to our worship,
    reminding us that each day is your gift,
    to be celebrated,
    savoured
    and, so far as we are able, lived to the full.
Help us, then, to offer you all we do today,
    rejoicing in all you have given
    and seeking to honour you in every part of life,
    through Jesus Christ our Lord.
Amen.

## 50

### *Mark 8:31-38*

Lord Jesus Christ,
    we are here because we want to honour you,
    to give you the acknowledgement and recognition you deserve.
Remind us that if we are truly to do so,
    our worship cannot be confined to these few moments
    but must spill over into daily life,
    and be shown there by our willingness to follow your way
    even when commitment proves costly.
Help us, then, to offer ourselves afresh to your service,
    and through meeting with you to find the resources we need
    to take up our cross
    and walk where you would lead us.
Amen.

## 51
### *Luke 24:44-53*

Lord Jesus Christ,
    Prince of Peace and King of kings,
    we bow in reverent praise,
    approaching in grateful homage
    to acknowledge your rule in our lives
    and to anticipate your reign over all.
Teach us today what it means to serve you,
    how best we might work for your kingdom.
Teach us to acclaim you
    not just in words but also in deeds,
    not just in worship but equally in life.
In your name we ask it.
Amen.

## 52
### *Matthew 25:14-30*

Lord Jesus Christ,
    teach us to anticipate the future
    by living faithfully for you in the present,
    using the gifts you have given us in your service.
Help us to worship you
    not just now but always,
    offering our time, energy, skills, money, love and witness to you,
    consecrating each to the work of your kingdom,
    for your name's sake.
Amen.

## 53

### *John 15:1-8*

Lord Jesus Christ,
  teach us to honour you
  not just through songs of worship,
  words of prayer
  or the outward practice of religion,
  but also through lives rooted in you,
  entwined with yours
  and producing fruits of the Spirit,
  our love, joy, peace and humility speaking to others of your goodness.
Dwell in us
  and unite us with you,
  that we may truly glorify your name,
  here;
  and everywhere.
Amen.

## 54

### *Luke 6:27-38*

Lord Jesus Christ,
  we come to you,
  remembering that you did not simply talk about love,
  but showed it, even on the cross,
  enduring agony and humiliation there
  as much for those who hated, persecuted and rejected you
  as for those who offered love in return.
Come again to us now and fill our hearts,
  for our words all too rarely lead to action,
  our talk of love seldom reinforced by deeds.
Receive the love we offer today,
  poor though it is,
  and, by your grace, increase it,
  so that, like yours, it may reach out to all –
  friends, enemies and neighbours alike –
  to the glory of your name.
Amen.

## 55
### *Luke 16:19-31*

Sovereign God,
    teach us, in our plenty,
    never to forget those who have less:
    the hungry and homeless,
    the poor and underprivileged,
    those denied the healthcare, education
    and resources we take for granted.
Broaden our horizons and enlarge our concern,
    so that our faith will not just be about what you do for us,
    but also about what we can do for others.
Remind us now that in serving them we serve you too,
    contributing in some way, however small,
    to the growth of your kingdom,
    here on earth as it is in heaven.
Amen.

## 56
### *Mark 6:14-29*

Sovereign God,
    open our hearts to everything you would say to us
    through your word and through those who speak it to us,
    however demanding it might be –
    however unpalatable the truth,
    demanding the challenge,
    humbling the experience
    or searching the questions we must face.
Speak to us and equip us to speak for you in turn,
    standing up for truth, right and justice,
    even though that may be equally demanding.
Give us strength and humility both to hear and to be your voice,
    through Jesus Christ our Lord.
Amen.

## 57

### *Matthew 7:21-29*

Living God,
    help us today, as we hear your word, to act upon it,
    consecrating our lives to you
    and committing ourselves again to your service.
Awaken us to all you would say,
    and teach us to build our lives upon Christ,
    our faith founded in him so that it is able to withstand
    whatever storms life may throw at it.
Speak now,
    and give us ears to hear,
    in his name.
Amen.

## 58

### *Matthew 21:23-32*

Lord Jesus Christ,
    teach us to recognise your authority in our lives
    and to respond freely to your call.
Show us what you would have us do
    and how you would have us serve.
Though the way may be hard
    and our inclination be to resist,
    inspire us, through love of you, to obey your summons
    and honour your will.
Above all, help us each day to recognise our need of you,
    and to receive again the love and pardon you delight to give.
We come now,
    hearts open in faith,
    lives offered in love,
    to your glory.
Amen.

**59**

*Matthew 10:24-39*

Sovereign God,
   we come to acknowledge you –
   to declare your greatness,
   profess our love
   and commit ourselves to your kingdom –
   but we know that this by itself amounts to little
   unless we acknowledge you equally in our daily life,
   declaring your name there also,
   professing our devotion
   and committing ourselves to your service
   with equal candour and sincerity.
Teach us to value you as much as you value us,
   through Jesus Christ our Lord.
Amen.

**60**

*Matthew 9:35-10:8*

Lord Jesus Christ,
   we come to you,
   the source of life,
   the bringer of peace,
   the giver of strength
   and the exemplar of love.
We *come* that we might be better equipped to *go* for you,
   to reach out in your name,
   carrying the good news to a bruised and broken world,
   testifying through our life and witness to your care for all.
Equip us here to serve you everywhere.
Amen.

## 61

### *Luke 10:1-11, 16-20*

Living God,
   through our being here today
   equip us to go out in your name,
   returning to our homes, families and friends,
   our places of work and leisure,
   and living out there,
   in word and deed,
   our faith in Christ.
Fill us here with the resources we need
   for faithful discipleship and witness,
   and so help us to discharge our calling
   and contribute to your kingdom,
   through Jesus Christ our Lord.
Amen.

## 62

### *Luke 10:38-42*

Sovereign God,
   help us, as we gather here once more,
   truly to focus on you;
   to direct our thoughts away
   from the pressures, demands and responsibilities of another week;
   away from anxieties and difficulties,
   trivial distractions and irrelevancies.
Help us to listen again to your word
   and hear what you would say to us,
   so that we might return to the daily routine,
   whatever it might hold,
   strengthened and encouraged,
   with deeper insight and a fresh perspective,
   through Jesus Christ our Lord.
Amen.

## 63
### *Luke 13:10-17*

Gracious God,
  teach us to recognise that neither religion nor worship
  are an end in themselves,
    but that each rather is designed to lead us closer to you
    and to help us work more effectively for your kingdom
    here on earth.
Save us from becoming too heavenly minded to be of any earthly use;
  from being so wrapped up in our own salvation
  that we neglect our responsibilities to others;
    or from focusing on the letter of the law rather than the spirit,
    reducing faith to rules and regulations rather than an affair of the heart,
    to outward show rather than inner experience.
Come now,
  and kindle true faith within us,
    through Jesus Christ our Lord.
Amen.

## 64
### *Luke 18:1-8*

Just and faithful God,
  we bring you our worship,
  knowing that you delight to receive us;
  we bring you our prayers,
  knowing that you are always ready to hear and answer.
Remind us once more of that truth today,
  and help us not just to assent to it with our minds
  but also to believe it in our hearts,
    so that we might worship you every day,
    and pray always,
    living each moment in relation to you,
    in the knowledge that you are always there
    and will respond.
Amen.

## 65
### *Luke 7:36-8:3*

Lord Jesus Christ,
 help us today,
 recognising the depth of your love and the extent of your mercy,
 to respond gladly,
 spontaneously
 and sacrificially,
 offering you heartfelt worship now
 and consecrating every moment to your service,
 so that we might honour you through the people we are
 and the lives we live.
May love and gratitude flow within us always,
 spilling over in generous and joyful response to you and others,
 to the glory of your name.
Amen.

# Easter

## 66

### *Matthew 28:1-10*

Great and wonderful God,
  today of all days we would praise you.
We would bring you our worship,
  our gratitude,
  our faith
  and our lives,
  offering them to you in joyful celebration
  at the victory you have won for us in Christ.
Grant, then, that everything we offer you today will speak of our joy,
  devotion
  and desire to follow Christ;
  to give ourselves to him as he gave himself for us.
Amen.

## 67

### *Luke 24:36b-48*

Sovereign God,
  rejoicing in the glorious fulfilment of your promises,
  your living, dying and rising among us through your Son,
  we bring you now our praise, thanksgiving,
  worship and commitment.
Open our lives afresh to your word
  and to the presence of the risen Christ.
Thrill us as we celebrate your faithfulness and sovereignty –
  the great victory of your love –
  and so may we go on our way today,
  your word on our lips,
  your joy in our eyes
  and your love in our hearts,
  through Jesus Christ our Lord.
Amen.

## 68
### *Mark 16:1-8*

Lord Jesus Christ,
    as Mary recognised you in the garden,
    as disciples met you on the Emmaus Road,
    as the Apostles encountered you standing among them
    and as Thomas knelt before you in homage,
    his doubts and questions overcome,
    so we would meet you now,
    our risen Lord and Saviour,
    conqueror of evil,
    triumphant over death.
We would acknowledge your greatness,
    acclaim your love,
    salute your victory
    and celebrate the new life you have given –
    the hope, joy, peace and blessing you have poured into our hearts.
Accept, then, our worship,
    and meet us through it.
Amen.

## 69
### *Luke 24:1-12*

Renewing and life-giving God,
    as we celebrate again your victory over death
    and triumph over evil,
    open our hearts today to the way you are able to change our lives
    and transform our world.
Remind us of your resurrection power all around us,
    bringing hope out of despair,
    joy out of sorrow,
    peace out of turmoil
    and love out of hatred,
    and in that faith may we live now and trust for the future,
    assured that nothing can defeat your purpose
    or deny the life you offer for all eternity,
    through Jesus Christ our Lord.
Amen.

## 70

*John 21:1-19*

Risen Lord,
    as we meet and greet you in worship,
    cause our spirits to leap and hearts to dance within us
    at the good news of your resurrection:
    the triumph of love,
    the victory of good,
    the conquest of death by life.
Enthral us again with that glorious message of the gospel,
    so that we will go on our way rejoicing,
    proclaiming the new life you have won for all,
    and making disciples in your name.
Amen.

## 71

*John 20:19-31*

Risen Saviour,
    though we have not seen the empty tomb and folded grave-clothes,
    the wounds in your hands and feet,
    or your physical presence among us,
    yet we believe,
    for we have tasted your love,
    experienced your power,
    known you deep within us through your Holy Spirit
    bringing joy, peace and fullness of life.
So we come today, simply to acclaim you,
    to bring our worship,
    to express our gratitude,
    to acknowledge you in praise, wonder and adoration,
    as our Lord and our God.
Amen.

## 72

### *Luke 24:13-35*

Lord Jesus Christ,
   as those who walked with you on the Emmaus Road
   recognised you in the breaking of bread,
   so may we recognise you now as we join in worship.
Grant that we too may meet with you,
   walk with you
   and talk with you,
   so that our hearts might burn within us
   as we go on our way, rejoicing.
Open our hearts, today and every day,
   to your living presence and life-giving power.
Amen.

## 73

### *John 20:19-31*

Lord Jesus Christ,
   meet with us now through your Spirit,
   reminding us of your living presence and risen power.
In a world where so much questions faith,
   denies love
   and threatens hope,
   may your resurrection life flow within us,
   convincing us of your eternal purpose:
   the blessings you hold in store –
   imperishable,
   unfading,
   kept in heaven –
   and may that assurance sustain us now and always.
Amen.

# Examples of faith

**74**

*Luke 7:1-10*

Lord Jesus Christ,
    inspire us and increase our faith as we worship you
    through everything you have accomplished in so many lives,
    responding to people's cry for help
    and ministering to their needs.
Inspire us through the faith of others:
    their trust in your power and purpose,
    their willingness to follow where you lead,
    their confidence in your unfailing love.
Inspire us through the way the good news continues to change lives,
    capturing the hearts of individuals the world over,
    their faith often putting ours to shame.
Speak to us now,
    so that we might trust you more,
    love you better
    and serve you more effectively,
    to the glory of your name.
Amen.

## 75

### *John 11:32-44*

Sovereign God,
    as part of your people in every place
    and every age –
    the great company in heaven
    and your Church here on earth –
    we join together to acknowledge your goodness
    and acclaim your power,
    seeking to honour, love and serve you in all we do.
Inspire us through the example of those who have gone before us –
    those who have kept the faith and run the race –
    so that we might follow in their footsteps,
    responding to your call,
    and living in such a way as to inspire in turn generations to come.
In Christ's name we pray.
Amen.

## 76

### *Luke 6:20-31*

God of all,
    conscious of your call to share in the inheritance of the saints,
    we ask you to help us live up to that honour.
Teach us through those whose names have gone down in history
    as examples of faith, courage, love,
    wisdom, goodness and compassion –
    their lives an inspiration to others,
    their witness a beacon of hope,
    their commitment a challenge to all.
Equip us, as we worship,
    to emulate in some small way their discipleship,
    to your glory.
Amen.

## 77

*Hebrews 11:32-12:2*

Eternal God
  for your faithfulness across the years,
  the guidance you have given
  and the love you have shown,
  we thank you.
For those whose lives bear testimony
  to your sovereign purpose and saving grace –
  inspiring, instructing, questioning and challenging –
  we give you praise.
Help us on this day of remembering
  to recall and learn from the heritage in which we stand –
  the eloquent testimony of lives lived for you,
  the innumerable examples of faith, courage, love and goodness.
Speak to us through them,
  so that we in turn might speak to others of you,
  through Jesus Christ our Lord.
Amen.

# Fellowship in Christ

### 78

*Mark 3:20-35*

Father God,
    draw us together here,
    united in faith, love and purpose,
    and with Christ and one another,
    having the same mind among us and same goal:
    to seek your kingdom and do your will.
Teach us what it means to be your children,
    your people,
    your family,
    and help us to honour you through honouring that calling.
Amen.

### 79

*John 17:1-11*

Sovereign God,
    we bring you this time of worship,
    not as the sum of our response but as a start,
    a small expression of our desire to honour you in all we do.
Teach us what that means:
    to recognise that, above all, you long for us to be one –
    with Christ,
    with you,
    and with your people everywhere –
    united in love,
    and striving together for the growth of your kingdom
    and the fulfilment of your will.
Live in us, that we might live for you,
    this day and always.
Amen.

## 80

### *1 Corinthians 12:12-31*

Lord of all,
    remind us, as we meet together today,
    of the wider fellowship to which we belong,
    and of the common faith, hope, love and purpose we share,
    in the name of Christ,
    with Christians across the world.
Give us a wider understanding of the many ways you work,
    the different experiences you give of your grace,
    and the diversity of people you choose to call and work through.
Save us from insular, judgemental or intolerant attitudes,
    and open our hearts instead to all we can give and receive
    within the family of your people.
Draw us closer to you,
    and so closer also to one another,
    through Jesus Christ our Lord.
Amen.

## 81

### *Matthew 16:13-20*

Loving Lord,
    once more we would confess our faith in you,
    acknowledging you as the Messiah,
    the Son of the living God,
    the one who sets us free and brings us life.
Help us to honour you
    not only in words but also through living faithfully as your people,
    your Body,
    your Church,
    working for and witnessing to your kingdom in word and deed.
Receive our worship,
    receive our faith,
    for your name's sake.
Amen.

# Fulfilment in Christ, true nature of

## 82
### *John 6:24-35*

Living God,
    in a world that looks for instant satisfaction,
    quick fixes,
    fast food,
    we turn again to you,
    seeking eternal fulfilment,
    lasting renewal
    and enduring nourishment through Christ.
Meet with us, we pray,
    and feed us once more,
    in body, mind and spirit.
Amen.

## 83
### *John 6:1-21*

Lord Jesus Christ,
    as you used a little to feed the multitude,
    so use this simple time of worship to feed us now,
    to nourish and sustain our faith and equip us for service.
Though our vision is small,
    our faith limited
    and our commitment a fraction of what it should be,
    accept what we offer,
    consecrating it by your grace
    and using it in ways beyond our expectations,
    to nurture us and others,
    filling our lives and theirs to overflowing.
Amen.

## 84

### *Luke 12:13-21*

Loving God,
    remind us again today of the nature of your kingdom,
    and help us to live accordingly.
Teach us that the treasures you give,
    whether earthly or heavenly,
    are not to be hoarded,
    stashed away for our own benefit,
    but to be shared,
    consecrated back to you in your service
    and to the benefit of others.
Grant us, then, generosity of spirit
    and spontaneity in devotion,
    so that we will understand the true meaning of riches
    and be ready to give as freely as we have received,
    through Jesus Christ our Lord.
Amen.

## 85

### *Mark 6:30-34, 53-56*

Living God,
    you know our needs better than we know them ourselves,
    you alone seeing into the heart
    and being able to offer real peace,
    enduring happiness
    and true fulfilment.
So we come,
    not to besiege you with requests
    or plague you with demands,
    but asking simply that you will work within us
    as you deem best,
    drawing us closer to you and increasing our faith.
Help us to focus above all on your kingdom and your righteousness,
    in the knowledge that you delight to give all we need
    and so much more,
    through Jesus Christ our Lord.
Amen.

## 86

### *John 6:56-69*

Lord,
  we find it hard to follow you sometimes,
  for your way is demanding,
  asking of us more than we feel we can give.
Yet though our faith may founder,
  so that we repeatedly fail you,
  we know in our hearts that you have the words of eternal life,
  and that without you our lives are ultimately empty,
  starved of real fulfilment.
So we come,
  seeking your mercy,
  and asking you to speak again,
  so that we might keep faith with you
  as surely as you keep faith with us to the end.
Amen.


## 87

### *Matthew 14:13-21*

Sovereign God,
  we bring you our spiritual hunger,
  our yearning for inner contentment,
  knowing that you alone can feed our souls,
  and do so in ways exceeding all our expectations.
Come, then, now,
  and reach out to all gathered here today,
  filling us with spiritual food –
  bread of life and living water –
  so that we may go on our way,
  nourished,
  filled,
  truly satisfied.
Amen.

# 88
## *Luke 16:1-13*

Living God,
    speak to us again of the things in life that really matter,
    that offer true joy and lasting fulfilment,
    for we so easily and often forget.
Remind us that the riches of this world
    can sometimes possess us rather than us them,
    and teach us, then, to use them wisely and generously,
    setting our hearts above all on treasures in heaven –
    the blessings of joy, hope, love and peace,
    life in abundance that you alone can offer.
Open our lives now to receive and respond,
    through Jesus Christ our Lord.
Amen.

# Grace of God in Christ

## 89

### *Luke 15:1-10*

Lord Jesus Christ,
   in the knowledge that you love us enough to seek us out,
   however often we go astray,
   that you are always ready to welcome us back,
   eager to forgive and forget,
   so we come now,
   summoned by your love,
   despite having erred and strayed like lost sheep,
   disobeying your will and rejecting your guidance in so much.
We come in penitence,
   but also assurance,
   knowing that you welcome us joyfully
   and without reserve.
Teach us, we pray, as we worship now,
   to value you as much as you value us.
Amen.

## 90

### *John 10:11-18*

Lord Jesus Christ,
   shepherd of the sheep,
   Lamb of God,
   we thank you that though we repeatedly err and stray,
   ignoring your voice and wandering far from your side,
   you not only seek us out,
   but also willingly lay down your life for us,
   freely giving that we might freely receive.
Equip us now to show our gratitude by following you more closely,
   trusting you more completely
   and obeying you more faithfully,
   so that our lives as well as our words may give honour to you,
   now and always.
Amen.

## 91
### *John 10:1-10*

Lord Jesus Christ,
   gracious shepherd,
   bringer of life,
   help us today once more to hear your voice and to respond,
   for, like lost sheep, we have gone astray,
   failing to follow where you lead or to trust you as we should.
Call us back,
   and show us again the right path,
   the way leading to true and abundant life,
   now and for all eternity.
Amen.

## 92
### *Matthew 9:9-13, 18-26*

Living God,
   we come to you,
   not because we have any claim on your goodness,
   or any right to expect your blessing,
   but because, in your love, you invite us here,
   delighting in our worship and glad to call us your children.
Yet we come too knowing that worship without response is empty,
   and words without deeds are hollow.
So we ask, by your grace,
   that you will deepen our knowledge of you
   and help us to love you as much as you love us,
   through Jesus Christ our Lord.
Amen.

## 93
### *Luke 18:9-14*

Gracious God,
   we do not come today under any illusions,
   with any sense that we are righteous,
   deserving
   or better than others.
We come because we know we are none of these –
   because our faults are all too clear to us,
   our weaknesses starkly apparent.
We come, then, throwing ourselves upon your mercy,
   begging for forgiveness,
   a fresh start,
   a new heart and right spirit within us.
Renew us, we pray,
   for we cannot do it ourselves.
Receive, accept and use us by your grace,
   for your kingdom.
Amen.

## 94
### *Luke 2:33-35*

Gracious God,
   though we have repeatedly forgotten you –
   going our own way,
   squandering your blessing
   and ignoring your will –
   teach us that you long still to welcome us back,
   your arms constantly outstretched to embrace us once more.
In that faith we come now,
   praising you for your goodness,
   acknowledging our many faults,
   thanking you for your mercy
   and seeking to love and serve you better.
Receive us
   and help us to open our hearts as wide to you
   as yours is open to us.
Amen.

## 95
### *Matthew 10:40-42*

Gracious God,
    we dare to draw near,
    not through any merit of our own
    but trusting in your great mercy –
    redeemed, renewed and restored through the love of Christ.
Set us free from all that holds us captive;
    we gladly surrender our lives to your service,
    to be used as you will.
As you have given,
    so we give back,
    in the name of Christ.
Amen.

## 96
### *Mark 2:1-12*

Sovereign God,
    we come to you conscious of all that is wrong in our lives,
    aware that we have no claim on your goodness
    nor any merit that might lead us to expect it.
Yet we come knowing that you are a God of love,
    slow to anger and swift to show mercy;
    a God who yearns to put the past behind us
    and to help us start again,
    if only we are truly sorry and sincerely wish it.
So, then, we dare to approach,
    trusting in your gracious love, so wonderfully revealed in Christ,
    and, in penitence, seeking forgiveness and new beginnings.
Through your Son, put your hand upon us,
    lift us up,
    restore us
    and send us on our way to live and work for you,
    in his name.
Amen.

## 97

### *Mark 1:40-45*

Lord Jesus Christ,
   reach out to us through this time of worship,
   and touch our lives
   with your cleansing, healing, restoring and renewing power.
Speak to us your word of forgiveness and peace,
   and, through your Spirit, move within us,
   encouraging,
   enthusing,
   equipping,
   enabling.
Encircle us in your love
   and enfold us in your grace,
   that we might find inner wholeness in body, mind and spirit,
   this and every day.
Amen.

## 98

### *Mark 7:24-37*

Lord,
   open our mouths that we might declare your praise;
   open our ears that we might hear your voice;
   open our hearts that our lives might be open in turn
   to you and others.
Teach us that your grace,
   your word
   and your love
   are for us and everyone,
   without partiality,
   your concern reaching to the ends of the earth –
   to people of every race, faith, culture and status –
   no one in your eyes of more or less worth than others.
Teach us, then, through our worship,
   how much you value us and everyone.
Amen.

## 99

### *Matthew 18:21-35*

Gracious God,
    we praise you that you welcome us into your presence
    despite all that is unworthy in our lives:
    all our faults, failings, falsehoods and faithlessness.
Speak to us through your willingness to forgive and go on forgiving,
    and so help us to forgive in turn,
    striving to heal broken relationships,
    mend quarrels,
    let bygones be bygones
    and start afresh.
Teach us through the example of Christ
    to show something of the mercy you have shown to us.
In his name we pray.
Amen.

## 100

### *Luke 13:1-9*

Loving God,
    conscious of our repeated disobedience to your will
    and our inability to serve you as we would like,
    we find it hard sometimes to believe you still have time for us,
    still delight in our presence and value our worship.
Yet you teach us that your nature is to forgive
    and go on forgiving.
Remind us of that now,
    and help us to come
    truly penitent
    but also truly confident that your love continues
    and your mercy endures.
Nurture, then, the faith you have sown within us,
    and, by your grace, help it to grow,
    so that our lives may fully bear fruit in your service.
Amen.

## 101

*Luke 23:26-49*

Lord Jesus Christ,
    we know that, whatever we give you,
    it can never begin to repay the price you paid to redeem us,
    nor ever earn the love you so freely showed,
    but we want to tell you how grateful we are
    for your awesome love and immense sacrifice.
We want to proffer a token of our love
    and a sign of our commitment;
    to respond to the joy you've brought us
    through offering heartfelt praise and committed service,
    honouring to you and pleasing in your sight.
Receive, then, the worship we bring,
    the faith we declare
    and the discipleship we offer,
    for, poor though they may be,
    we offer them with body, mind and soul
    humbly to you.
Amen.

# Growth: in faith
# and understanding

## 102

*John 20:19-31*

Risen Christ,
  meet with us afresh today,
  so that the worship we share may be *our* worship,
  the faith we proclaim be *our* faith
  and the joy we celebrate be *our* joy.
Come among us through your Spirit
  and lead us into deeper knowledge of the truth,
  so that the good news,
  declared across countless generations and in countless places,
  may be good news for us today,
  burning within us
  and stirring us to respond in grateful praise,
  loving service
  and joyful witness,
  to the glory of your name.
Amen.

## 103

### *John 3:1-17*

God of love,
   we come in faith,
   trusting in your word,
   rejoicing in your gift of life,
   now and for all eternity,
   but we come also yearning to know you better,
   to understand more and to fathom deeper mysteries.
Move among us now, through your Spirit,
   bringing new life to birth.
Open our hearts to all you would say and do,
   in us and through us.
In Christ's name we pray.
Amen.

## 104

### *John 1:43-51*

Lord Jesus Christ,
   you know us better than we know ourselves,
   seeing us as we really are,
   with all our faults and limitations,
   our quirks and weaknesses,
   yet giving your all for us in love.
Help us simply to know you *better* –
   glimpsing a little more clearly who you are
   in all your glory, greatness, love and compassion –
   so that, in love, we might give back to you in love,
   offering our worship now,
   our time today
   and our discipleship always,
   in grateful response.
Amen.

## 105

### *Matthew 13:24-30, 36-43*

God of justice and truth, yet also of love and mercy,
    focus our thoughts on you,
    so that we are open to fresh insights into truth,
    new horizons in faith
    and a deeper understanding of your purpose.
Help us to stand up against evil
    and to work together for good,
    recognising that you yearn to redeem all
    and do not willingly let go of anyone.
So may we contribute to your kingdom's growth among us now,
    through Jesus Christ our Lord.
Amen.

## 106

### *John 1:1-18*

Lord Jesus Christ,
    we know you,
    but not as well as we should do;
    we have received you into our hearts,
    but not as fully as we ought to have done;
    we have believed in your name,
    but not as completely as you or we would like.
Dwell among us now, through your Spirit,
    and grant us grace upon grace,
    so that, glimpsing more of your glory and grasping more of truth,
    we will open our hearts again to you,
    and welcome you with body, mind and soul
    as the Word made flesh,
    the Light of the World,
    the source and giver of life.
To you be praise and glory,
    now and always.
Amen.

## 107
### *John 3:1-17*

Eternal God,
 Father, Son and Holy Spirit,
 Lord of the past, the present and the future,
 with body, mind and spirit we worship you.
Open our eyes to your presence around us,
 our hearts to your love within us
 and our lives to your purpose beyond us.
Meet us now,
 and help us to catch a greater sense of who and what you are,
 so that we might praise you
 not just in these moments set aside
 but every moment of every day,
 to the glory of your name.
Amen.

## 108
### *Luke 2:41-52*

Father God,
 as you drew Jesus even as a child to your house,
 to seek you there and learn more of your will,
 so help us to sense your hand drawing us here today,
 to guide, challenge, nourish and nurture,
 opening up new experiences of your love
 and fresh insights into your will.
Grant that we might approach you now,
 not out of duty or habit
 but hungry to meet with you once more,
 to hear your voice
 and to answer your call,
 through Jesus Christ our Lord.
Amen.

## 109
### *Romans 11:33-36*

Gracious God,
   open our eyes to your goodness, greatness, love and mercy,
   for so often we fail to see as clearly as we should.
We close our eyes to what we would rather not face,
   allow the concerns of each day
   to obscure the wonder of your presence
   or simply take for granted what has become so familiar.
Touch our lives now as we worship you,
   and grant us, through all we share,
   deeper insight,
   a greater vision
   and a clearer picture of who and what you are.
In Christ's name we pray.
Amen.

# Growth: in grace

## 110

### *Matthew 21:33-46*

Loving God,
  help us, as we worship you, to look honestly at ourselves
  and recognise where we fail you,
  where our lives fall short,
  where our commitment is weak,
  where the harvest is poor.
Come to us afresh,
  and bring growth in grace,
  fresh shoots of the Spirit,
  signs of new life.
In your mercy, nurture our faith,
  so that we might bear fruit for you,
  reflecting your love
  and living to your praise and glory,
  through Jesus Christ our Lord.
Amen.

## 111

### *John 4:5-42*

God of all,
  we thirst to know you better,
  to grow closer to you each day.
Reach out now and speak your word of life.
Equip us to worship you in Spirit and in truth,
  so that your grace may pour upon us,
  and your love well up in our hearts,
  refreshing, reviving and renewing,
  satisfying body, mind and soul.
Meet us here, in all our weakness,
  and grant us the living water that you alone can give,
  through Jesus Christ our Lord.
Amen.

## 112

*John 17:20-26*

Gracious God,
   open our hearts afresh today
   to the fullness of life you want us to experience,
   not only in eternity but also here and now –
   life lived in union with you,
   in harmony with your will
   and in the light of your love.
Draw us closer to your side,
   so that whatever separates us from you,
   undermining the unity you want us to enjoy,
   will be overcome,
   our lives in consequence bearing witness to you,
   so that others in turn
   might know and believe in you for themselves,
   through Jesus Christ our Lord.
Amen.

## 113

*John 16:4b-15, 26-27*

Spirit of God,
   fill us now as we worship you.
Sanctify our listening and thinking,
   our giving and doing,
   so that all we offer and all we are
   may reach up to you and out to others,
   in impulsive praise and joyful service.
Teach, equip, guide and inspire us
   this and every day.
Amen.

# 114

*Matthew 15:21-28*

Gracious God,
    remind us as we worship you
    that you see not the outside but the person beneath;
    that you look beyond appearances to the thoughts of the heart.
Save us, then, from empty show or superficial piety,
    and teach us to approach you instead in faith and humility,
    knowing that your love extends to all who truly seek you,
    through Jesus Christ our Lord.
Amen.

# 115

*Matthew 5:13-20*

Lord Jesus Christ,
    as you taught the crowds on the mountaintop,
    so now teach us as we gather in your name.
Prompt us through your Spirit,
    that we might hear and understand your word.
Help us to listen and learn,
    reflecting on what you say to us and applying it to our lives,
    so that our words and deeds might bear witness to you,
    your light shining through us,
    to the glory of God the Father.
Amen.

## 116
### *John 17:6-19*

Sovereign and saving God,
    sanctify our hearts by your touch,
    so that the flawed worship we offer
    may nonetheless be pleasing to you
    and speak to us.
Sanctify us in truth,
    so that we will know, love and serve you better.
Sanctify all we are and all we do,
    so that, consecrating our lives to your service,
    we may live each moment in the light of your love,
    your grace shining through our witness as light to the world,
    drawing together all people to you,
    through Jesus Christ our Lord.
Amen.

## 117
### *John 6:35, 41-51*

Loving God,
    we cannot see you except through Christ;
    we cannot come to Christ unless you draw us to him;
    and so we approach you again,
    recognising our need,
    our dependence on you,
    and asking you to create and increase our faith,
    helping us to believe not just nominally
    but with body, mind and soul,
    with our whole heart and being.
Hear us
    and answer our prayer,
    through Jesus Christ our Lord.
Amen.

## 118

*Mark 6:1-13*

Lord Jesus Christ,
    save us from losing sight of why we are here;
    from speaking and failing to listen,
    from giving and forgetting to receive,
    from praying and refusing to hear,
    from looking but failing to seek.
Open our lips to praise you,
    our eyes to see you,
    our ears to hear you
    and our lives to serve you,
    to the glory of your name.
Amen.

## 119

*John 5:1-9*

Sovereign God,
    come among us,
    upon us
    and within us through your Holy Spirit,
    so that we may be equipped both to know your will
    and to do it.
Grant us an inner experience of your presence,
    so that your word might be unfolded,
    your peace given,
    your love nurtured
    and your power imparted,
    such that we may honour you not just here and now
    but in every place and at all times,
    through keeping your commands and observing your will.
In Christ's name we pray.
Amen.

# 120

*Luke 11:1-13*

Almighty God,
 help us to grasp more clearly today that,
 for all your purity, holiness, righteousness and power,
 you call us your children,
 wanting us to relate to you as our Father –
 one who values every one of us,
 who takes pleasure in our presence
 and who delights to give us good things.
Teach us to live in the light of that truth,
 turning to you each day
 for the guidance and blessing you so long to provide,
 seeking above all the indwelling of your Spirit,
 through which *you* live in us and *we* can live in you.
In Christ's name we pray.
Amen.

# Holy Week

*see also* Lord's Supper

## 121

*Mark 15:21-39*

Lord Jesus Christ,
  we come today to remember,
  to marvel,
  to give thanks
  and to worship.
We come to recall the agony you endured,
  the sorrow, humiliation and despair,
  and to celebrate the fact that you bore all this for people like us –
  weak, foolish, faithless –
  people who repeatedly fail you and betray your awesome love.
Help us to glimpse today, through all we share,
  more of what you have done for us,
  to appreciate all that it cost you
  and to respond with thankful, joyful hearts,
  and lives consecrated to your service.
In your name we pray.
Amen.

## 122

*Matthew 26:36-56*

Lord Jesus Christ,
  we remember today how you were betrayed,
  abandoned,
  denied,
  your disciples' commitment evaporating
  as the heat was turned on.
We come, conscious that our faith is likewise flawed and frail,
  strong enough when little is asked of us
  but vulnerable if put to the test.

Remind us, however, that you went to the cross
   knowing our weakness,
   ready to die for us despite our faults.
In that knowledge we come now –
   humble,
   thankful,
   joyful.
Receive our praise.
Amen.

# 123

## *Matthew 27:32-54*

Lord Jesus Christ,
   like those who stood at the foot of the cross,
   watching as you writhed in agony,
   cried out in despair
   and breathed your last,
   help us today to glimpse the astonishing extent of your love,
   the immensity of your sacrifice
   and the awful reality of what you suffered.
Help us through that to understand how much you love us
   and how much you were ready to bear
   to overcome everything that keeps us from you,
   and may that knowledge feed our faith,
   deepen our discipleship
   and reinforce our resolve to follow you,
   by your grace,
   and in your strength.
  Amen.

## 124
### *John 15:9-17*

Living Lord,
  as we prepare again to celebrate your resurrection,
  help us also to keep in mind what made it possible:
  your readiness to endure the agony and anguish of the cross;
  your love so great
  that you were willing to lay down your life for our sake.
Write that truth once more in our hearts today,
  so that the worship we offer now
  will be reinforced by the love we show in turn,
  to you,
  to each other
  and to all.
In your name we pray.
Amen.

# Hope, eternal nature of

**125**

*Mark 13:1-8*

Lord Jesus Christ,
  we look to you for wisdom and discernment,
  strength and support,
  guidance and inspiration.
Reveal to us, as we worship you,
  more of your sovereign purpose and gracious will,
  and help us to anticipate your kingdom
  through working for it now,
  trusting in your love despite all that fights against it,
  confident that, in the fullness of time,
  you will come again to reign here on earth,
  as you do in heaven.
Equip us, then, to stand firm,
  and, in a world of turmoil and strife,
  to keep faith that, though all else may fail,
  you will not.
Amen.

## 126

### *Luke 20:27-38*

Sovereign God,
  refresh our faith as we worship you;
  rekindle our trust in your eternal purpose,
  our confidence that nothing can separate us from your love.
Though we struggle to get our heads round the mechanics
  of resurrection
  or the nature of the kingdom of heaven,
  teach us to focus on what we know and understand –
  our daily experience of your love,
  the blessings you give us here and now,
  the light, joy and peace you have put into our hearts.
Remind us that these are but a taste of things to come;
  that whatever we have received,
  you hold yet greater things in store,
  through Jesus Christ our Lord.
Amen.

## 127

### *Luke 21:5-19*

Living God,
  teach us to trust in your future
  and to keep faith in the final dawning of your kingdom,
  but save us from dwelling on such things,
  indulging in futile speculation
  or being taken in by the conjectures of others.
Teach us, rather, to live faithfully for you,
  serving and honouring you through following the way of Christ
  despite everything that deflects us from it.
Help us to consecrate the present to you,
  and to leave all else in your hands,
  through Jesus Christ our Lord.
Amen.

# Humility

## 128
### *Mark 10:2-16*

Living God,
    through this time of worship touch our being in every part:
    our attitudes,
    relationships,
    thoughts, words and deeds;
    the way we respond to you and others,
    the way we love and live.
Teach us, in childlike humility,
    to value all,
    respect all
    and work for the good of all,
    recognising that everyone you have made is precious to you,
    the work of your hands,
    with a special place in your heart.
Reach out now
    and put your Spirit within us,
    through Jesus Christ our Lord.
Amen.

## 129

### *Luke 19:1-10*

Lord Jesus Christ,
    give us today true eagerness and genuine determination
    to see and hear you for ourselves.
Give us honesty and humility when we hear your call
    to admit our faults and be truly sorry;
    to welcome you into our lives
    and do what we can to make amends,
    not to earn your favour
    but to demonstrate our gratitude for all you have done,
    and our desire to offer you faithful service in return.
Draw near,
    meet us,
    and work afresh in our lives,
    to your glory.
Amen.

## 130

### *Mark 9:30-37*

Lord Jesus Christ,
    Lord of all yet servant of all,
    teach us your way of gentleness and humility,
    so that we in turn may serve you and others.
Nurture us now, as we worship you,
    and put a new nature within us –
    a childlike innocence and sincerity,
    enthusiasm and spontaneity,
    trust and dependence –
    so that, open to fresh horizons,
    we may be ready to learn more of you,
    to grow in grace,
    and to respond obediently to your call in faith and love,
    to your glory.
Amen.

## 131
### *Mark 10:35-45*

Sovereign God,
    teach us to follow you not for our ends but yours,
    seeking first your glory and the furtherance of your kingdom.
Remind us that the way of Christ
    turns our understanding of life upside down,
    freedom being found in service,
    greatness in humility,
    strength in weakness,
    and life through dying to self.
Reveal to us more of what that means,
    so that we might be equipped
    to honour you here in our worship,
    and each day in our lives,
    through Jesus Christ our Lord.
Amen.

# Kingship of Christ

## 132
### *Luke 24:44-53*

Saviour Christ,
    King of kings and Lord of lords,
    we want today to offer more than well-intentioned routine,
    more than hymns and prayers,
    words and music,
    preaching and teaching.
We want to offer worship,
    praise,
    adoration,
    bubbling up from within,
    welling up,
    spilling over,
    expressing our love and gratitude,
    and offering our lives back to you in joyful response.
Come among us now, through your Spirit,
    and reveal your glory.
Fill and thrill us afresh with your grace,
    and help us to bless your name,
    as you have blessed us in so much.
Amen.

## 133

### *Luke 24:44-53*

Lord Jesus Christ,
    remind us through this day
    that you are King, but not of this world;
    that you rule, but not through force;
    that you invite our respect, but do not demand it;
    that you are the Lord of lords, but servant of all.
Give us a deeper understanding of your kingdom
    and a firmer grasp of your will.
Teach us the way of humility and the path of love,
    so that we may honour you now in worship
    and each day in service,
    to your glory.
Amen.

## 134

### *Matthew 25:31-46*

Lord Jesus Christ,
    humble yet exalted,
    servant yet sovereign,
    teach us afresh today that through honouring others
    we honour you,
    and through serving them we serve you.
Awaken us to your presence all around us
    and to your call, especially in the cry of the needy,
    and in responding to the hungry,
    the sick,
    the lonely
    and the oppressed,
    may we respond also to you.
Reach out to us in mercy,
    that we might reach out to you and to them in love.
Amen.

## 135

### *Matthew 27:11-54*

Lord Jesus Christ,
    we come to declare your greatness,
    to acclaim you as King,
    to profess our allegiance
    and to seek your will for our lives.
Instruct us through this service,
    so that, glimpsing the true meaning of power
    and the nature of your rule,
    we may commit ourselves more fully to you
    and gain a clearer understanding of your purpose for all.
Amen.

## 136

### *Luke 19:28-40*

Lord Jesus Christ,
    teach us today not just to welcome you as King,
    but also to commit ourselves to your kingdom,
    putting our lives at your disposal for you to use as you will.
Take our faith, witness and service,
    our gifts, time and money,
    our thoughts, words and deeds,
    and use all to fulfil your royal purpose,
    to your glory.
Amen.

## 137

*Mark 11:1-11*

Lord Jesus Christ,
   we come today
   remembering how crowds joyfully welcomed you into Jerusalem,
   but remembering also how a mob called there for your death,
   the space of a few days making such a difference
   to the response you received.
Help us, then, as we greet and acclaim you,
   to search ourselves and examine the homage we offer,
   so that the faith we profess today will be as real tomorrow
   and every day
   as it is now,
   to the glory of your name.
Amen.

## 138

*John 18:33-37*

Lord Jesus Christ,
   despised,
   rejected,
   yet risen and enthroned on high,
   reign in our hearts and rule in our lives.
Grant that, just as we extol you now –
   singing your praises,
   giving you glory
   and declaring our commitment,
   so we may similarly acclaim you always –
   praising, glorifying and serving you
   through obedience to your will,
   in thought, word and deed.
In your name we ask it.
Amen.

## 139

*Luke 23:33-43*

Lord Jesus Christ,
   crowned with thorns yet crowned with glory,
   lifted up on a cross yet exalted on high,
   crucified as a criminal yet honoured as Lord,
   sealed in a tomb yet triumphant over death,
   remind us again today of your transforming power
   and renewing love;
   the way you overturn the wisdom of this world,
   bringing victory out of defeat,
   joy out of sorrow
   and hope out of despair.
Teach us again, as we worship you,
   that you are able to change our lives and our world,
   bringing light into our darkness,
   wholeness in our brokenness.
Reach out in love
   and work your miracle of grace.
Amen.

# Lent

## 140

### *Mark 1:9-15*

Lord Jesus Christ,
    as you wrestled in the wilderness with temptation,
    with the nature of your calling
    and your ability to meet what it would cost you,
    so help us today
    and throughout this time of Lent
    to hear your voice,
    to understand what you ask of us
    and to consider our response.
Fasten our thoughts on you,
    and direct all that we do,
    so that we might grow in grace
    and stand firm in faith,
    able to resist whatever might cause us to fall.
In your name we pray.
Amen.

## 141

### *Matthew 4:1-11*

Search us, O God, and know our thoughts.
Examine us and reveal our faults.
Cleanse us and make us new.
Touch us and make us whole.
Equip us and give us strength.
Meet us and speak your word.
Hear us and accept our worship,
    in Jesus' name.
Amen.

## 142

### *1 John 1:5-10*

Redeemer God,
    we come in this season of Lent,
    conscious of our weakness,
    dismayed by the feebleness of our faith,
    and yearning to show penitence
    at our inability to serve you as we would and should.
But we come also gladly
    and with confidence,
    knowing that you are a gracious God,
    slow to punish and swift to forgive,
    always looking to bless, restore and renew.
Remind us of that truth as we worship you,
    both now and in the days ahead,
    so that true repentance may be matched by true thanksgiving,
    and sorrow at our many faults be balanced
    by rejoicing at your inestimable love and mercy.
In Christ's name we pray.
Amen.

## 143

### *Luke 4:1-13*

Living God,
    we would offer this day in worship,
    but we are so easily led astray,
    our minds preoccupied with other concerns,
    our attention caught by trivia,
    our sense of expectation eroded by familiarity.
We would offer our lives in service,
    but it is a similar story,
    our faith so often suffocated by the cares of each day,
    our discipleship put second to what can never truly satisfy,
    our relationship with you taken for granted
    and allowed to stagnate.

Through this time together,
   and this season,
   call us back to you.
Remind us of essentials,
   challenge us concerning our priorities
   and restore us to your side,
   so that when temptation comes
   we will stay as true to you as you are true to us.
Amen.

## 144

### *Hebrews 4:14-16*

God of all,
   conscious of our weakness but trusting in your grace
   we come now before you,
   consecrating this service,
   this day
   and this season to you.
Grant that today,
   and this time of Lent,
   may draw us closer to you,
   so that, acknowledging the frailty of our faith
   and limitations of our discipleship,
   we might find pardon and cleansing,
   guidance and inspiration,
   strength and blessing,
   equipping us to walk more faithfully in the days ahead,
   through Jesus Christ our Lord.
  Amen.

## 145

### *2 Corinthians 13:5-10*

Eternal God,
    as we worship you today and throughout this season of Lent,
    help us to recognise all that is wrong in our lives,
    all that separates us from you and others,
    all that obstructs your purpose,
    leads us into temptation
    and causes us to fall.
Help us, prayerfully and humbly, to examine ourselves
    and honestly acknowledge our faults,
    not so that we might wallow in self-pity or indulge in false piety,
    but so that we may receive cleansing, healing and forgiveness –
    renewal in body, mind and spirit,
    through Jesus Christ our Lord.
Amen.

# Light, of Christ

## 146

### *John 19:25-27*

Gracious God,
   remind us again as we worship you of how much you love us
   and how much you are willing to do for our sakes.
Teach us to appreciate the full extent of your devotion
   and to respond by consecrating our lives to Christ,
   so that his grace may flow through us,
   leading us out of darkness into his marvellous light.
Shine upon us,
   within us
   and through us,
   for we ask it in his name.
Amen.

## 147

### *Matthew 2:1-12*

Lord Jesus Christ,
   Light of the World,
   shine in our hearts,
   banishing all that obscures your goodness
   and darkens our lives.
Illuminate this time of worship,
   so that in every part it will draw us closer to you,
   revealing more of your purpose
   and unfolding more of your grace.
Come to us
   as we come now to you,
   and flood our lives with the radiance of your love
   so that it may shine not just *in* us
   but also *through* us –
   a light set upon a hill
   bringing glory to you.
Amen.

## 148
### *Matthew 4:12-23*

Sovereign God,
  without your light in our lives we walk in darkness,
  denied the joy, peace, hope, strength and guidance
  that you alone can give.
So we ask, through this time of worship,
  that the light of Christ might break yet more fully into our hearts
  and shine more brightly through our lives,
  to your glory.
Amen.

## 149
### *Matthew 2:1-12*

Lord Jesus Christ,
  hope of your people,
  hope of your world,
  touch now our lives as we gather before you.
Shine in our hearts,
  illumine our minds
  and light up our spirits,
  so that we will grasp more clearly
  the hope you give us:
  the assurance of your love
  and the joy of life in all its fullness,
  here now
  and for all eternity.
Amen.

# Lord's Supper

## 150

### 1 Corinthians 11:23-32

Lord Jesus Christ,
   you invite us here to break bread and share wine,
   in remembrance of your death,
   in celebration of your continuing life
   and in anticipation of your coming in glory.
Help us, as we share together, to do all those:
   to recall the awful and awesome cost of our redemption,
   to recognise your presence with us now through your Spirit,
   and to trust you for the future, keeping faith in your kingdom.
Nourish and nurture us with the bread of life and your word of truth,
   now and always.
Amen.

## 151

### John 6:51-58

Lord Jesus Christ,
   remind us through the symbol of bread
   of your body broken for us –
   bread of life,
   offered freely,
   lovingly,
   to us,
   to all.
Help us, then, as we worship and break bread together,
   to feed on you in our hearts by faith,
   receiving the life-giving nourishment that you so graciously offer,
   so that we may grow in strength,
   progress in faith,
   and mature in discipleship,
   to the glory of your name.
Amen.

## 152

### *Matthew 22:1-14*

Living God,
    we come at your invitation
    to celebrate,
    to receive,
    to eat at your table and be filled.
Help us to prepare our hearts and minds to receive all you offer
    and to clothe ourselves with your gifts of love,
    joy,
    peace,
    goodness,
    compassion
    and humility –
    whatever is pleasing and honouring to you –
    freely offering ourselves in the service of Christ,
    who freely gave so much for us.
Amen.

## 153

### *Mark 14:17-25*

Lord Jesus Christ,
    remind us today that you were broken for us –
    that you endured the agony of the cross to set us free
    and the darkness of death to bring us life –
    but remind us also that you were broken for many,
    your love extending to all
    in every place and time.
Reach out, then,
    and touch our worship now
    and throughout this holy season,
    so that we in turn might reach out to others,
    in your name
    and with your love.
Amen.

# Love, giving and receiving

## 154
### *Matthew 5:38-48*

Living God,
  we want to love you,
  we want to love others,
  but we're not very good at doing either.
Today, as we worship you,
  teach us more of what love really means.
Speak to us through Christ,
  and, through your Holy Spirit, equip us to follow his way,
  turning the other cheek,
  going the extra mile,
  praying for our enemies,
  giving without counting the cost.
Help us to love as fully as you love us,
  to your glory.
Amen.

## 155

### *Matthew 20:1-16*

Sovereign and saving God,
   for your mercy that redeems us
   and your love that welcomes us
   we praise you.
We deserve nothing
   and yet you gave all to bring us life,
   now and always.
Help us today to grasp the extent of your love,
   the breadth of your purpose
   and the scope of your grace –
   to recognise that no one is beyond your mercy
   or outside your concern.
Teach us, then, to be generous in our dealings with others,
   as you have dealt so generously with us,
   through Jesus Christ our Lord.
Amen.

## 156

### *Luke 10:25-37*

Living God,
   help us to understand more clearly today
   that loving you must show itself in loving others;
   that commitment should spill over into compassion,
   faith into works
   and prayer into service.
Open our eyes to the needs of our neighbours,
   both near and far,
   and help us wherever possible
   to express something of your care and concern for all,
   ministering to them in the name of Christ.
Amen.

## 157

### *Mark 12:28-34*

Sovereign God,
  remind us again today of what really matters to you,
  what alone breathes life into worship and service,
  all else being as nothing without it –
  the gift of love.
Teach us that around this greatest of attributes
  revolve the two greatest commandments –
  to love you
  and others –
  and so, we pray, put your love within us,
  so that it may underlie all we offer now
  and do always.
Fill our lives to overflowing,
  so that we will truly love you
  with all our heart, understanding and strength,
  and love our neighbour as ourselves,
  through Jesus Christ our Lord.
Amen.

## 158

### *John 12:1-8*

Lord of all,
  fill us with love,
  so that we might truly worship you.
May all we say, think and do come from the heart,
  inspired by love in return,
  and offered to you not because it's expected of us
  but because we yearn to express our devotion,
  to show you how much you mean to us
  and how thankful we are
  for the difference you've made to our lives.
Amen.

## 159

### *Luke 14:1, 7-14*

Sovereign God,
    teach us to love without demanding we are loved first,
    to serve without expecting service in return,
    to give without seeking recompense,
    to show compassion to others
    even when they care nothing about us.
Remind us, as we worship you,
    that you have shown just such love to us in Christ,
    just such service, generosity and compassion,
    and, by your grace, grant that something of you
    may shine through us,
    to the glory of your name.
Amen.

## 160

### *Matthew 22:34-46*

Sovereign God,
    remind us through this time of worship of the essentials of faith –
    love for you and love for others –
    and through our being here today
    nurture such love within our lives.
Touch our hearts through your Spirit,
    and renew us through the grace of Christ,
    so that our devotion to you and to the good of others
    may be as real as that you so faithfully show us.
Help us now truly to love you with heart and mind and soul,
    and to love our neighbour as ourselves.
Amen.

## 161
### *Mark 5:21-43*

Sovereign God,
    give us a sense of your nearness as we worship you,
    so that we might hear your voice
    and learn more of your love in Christ.
Teach us through his life and ministry,
    and through all those who, across the years,
    have experienced his power
    and felt the touch of his hand in their lives,
    to respond in turn,
    bringing our broken lives and broken world to him,
    and opening all to his healing, restoring and life-giving love.
Amen.

# New beginnings

## 162

### *Mark 1:29-39*

Gracious God,
    may the good news of Jesus Christ
    thrill us again as we worship you;
    may the message of his saving power kindle fresh faith within us;
    may the touch of his hand bring us new beginnings;
    may the experience of his love send us on our way,
    restored,
    made whole.
Open our lives to the wonder of the gospel,
    so that, experiencing the joy and fulfilment it brings,
    we may share it with others,
    helping them too to know the truth
    and experience your love for themselves,
    to the glory of your name.
Amen.

## 163

### *Matthew 2:13-23*

Lord Jesus Christ,
    we come to you in worship,
    rejoicing that you made your home among us,
    sharing our life and death in order to bring us new birth,
    forgiveness
    and a fresh start.
Come again now, we ask,
    and through your grace work within us,
    absolving all that is wrong in our lives and unworthy of your love.
Draw us closer to you each day
    and lead us in the way of truth,
    so that, growing in faith,
    we might know and do your will,
    to the glory of God the Father.
Amen.

# Pentecost

### 164
*Acts 2:1-21*

Spirit of God,
  come among us,
  move among us,
  work among us.
Breathe life into our worship,
  love into our hearts
  and light into our witness.
Come as fire,
  refining and cleansing.
Come as the wind,
  blowing the cobwebs from our lives.
Come as a dove,
  enfolding us in your peace.
Come *to* us,
  move *in* us,
  work *through* us,
  now and always.
Amen.

## 165
### *John 14:8-27*

Holy Spirit,
   touch again the worship we bring you.
Speak through the hymns we will sing,
   the words we will hear,
   the prayers we will offer
   and the fellowship we will share,
   so that your fruits may grow within us,
   your gifts be released,
   your power displayed
   and your counsel given.
Open our hearts to all you would say
   and all you would do among us,
   through Jesus Christ our Lord.
Amen.

# Special services

## 166
### Baptism/Dedication of a Child
#### *Matthew 18:1-14*

Living God,
    Father of all,
    we come today thanking you for the gift of this child,
    with all the joy yet demands,
    expectations yet responsibilities,
    surrounding him/her.
We come also thanking you for the gift of eternal life,
    new birth in Christ,
    recognising equally the blessing yet challenge,
    reward yet cost,
    that this involves too.
Receive today the commitment that will be expressed
    and vows made,
    and, by your grace, lead each of us to discover in life now
    the joy of life in all its fullness –
    your gracious gift through Jesus Christ our Lord.
Amen.

## 167

## Believers' Baptism

*Acts 8:26-40*

Lord Jesus Christ,
  as we share today in this service of commitment –
  this symbol of new beginnings
  and celebration of your great mercy and love –
  call us all to deeper faith,
  greater trust,
  stronger commitment
  and truer devotion.
Remind us of the fresh start you have won for us,
  the fulfilment you offer
  and the blessings you long to impart,
  and through sharing each day in your death and resurrection,
  putting off the old and rising to the new,
  may we know, honour, love and serve you more faithfully,
  to the glory of your name.
Amen.

## 168

## Christian Aid Week

*James 2:14-26*

Lord of all,
  remind us again today
  of the special place the poor have in your heart,
  the concern you have for the oppressed and exploited,
  the homeless and refugees,
  the sick and suffering –
  all who are denied justice and hope,
  a fair share in the good things you have given.
Remind us of this,
  so that they may have a special place in our hearts also,
  their plight rousing us to similar compassion,
  similar concern
  and a desire in some way to help make a difference.

Teach us, through this service, to appreciate our plenty
and our responsibilities to others;
to understand that it is in serving them that we serve you;
and may that knowledge inspire us
to work with renewed zeal for your kingdom,
striving to bring it closer here on earth
as it is in heaven.
In Christ's name we ask it.
Amen.

## 169

## Christian Burial

*Revelation 21:1-5; 22:1-5*

Eternal God,
draw near today as we worship you,
so that this time of sorrow and heartache
will also be one of joy and hope;
this day of endings also one of new beginnings;
this acknowledgement of death also a celebration of life,
lived to the full and with more yet to come.
Reach out into the pain of this moment,
giving the assurance that those who mourn will be comforted,
that your purpose continues,
and that nothing finally can ever separate us
from your love in Christ.
Help us, then,
giving thanks for what has been
and looking forward to what shall be,
to receive your peace, strength, help and love now,
through Jesus Christ our Lord.
Amen.

# 170

## Christian Marriage

*1 Corinthians 13:1-13*

Gracious God,
    through this joyful occasion today,
    speak to everyone present of your great gift of love:
    the love we share in our daily relationships,
    that unites us as your people,
    that you call us to show to others,
    that you have so freely and wonderfully shown in Christ.
Move in our hearts,
    and fill us with that most precious of gifts:
    a love that binds us together,
    enriching, empowering, restoring and renewing;
    and may that shape our lives –
    bride, groom, friend or family –
    bringing us lasting joy,
    true happiness,
    not just today but every day,
    through Jesus Christ our Lord.
Amen.

# 171

## Church Anniversary

*Hebrews 13:7-8*

Loving God,
    we come again into your presence,
    recognising the goodness and love you have so faithfully shown,
    your interest and involvement both in our daily lives
    and in our life together as your people.
We come,
    thanking you for the way you have prompted and provided,
    equipped and enabled,
    inspired and instructed,
    nurtured and nourished across the years.

Speak again now, through this time of celebration and thanksgiving,
    as we remember the past and anticipate the future.
Uplift us through the hymns and songs we shall share,
    challenge us through the message proclaimed,
    hear and answer us through the prayers we offer,
    and accept all we bring in grateful response.
Rekindle our faith,
    revive our vision
    and renew our life,
    through Jesus Christ our Lord.
Amen.

# 172

## Education Sunday

### *Matthew 5:1-12*

Lord Jesus Christ,
    remembering how you taught the multitudes
    throughout your ministry,
    patiently bringing home your message
    through stories and illustrations drawn from daily life,
    so we come today to pray for teachers and pupils –
    all who seek to impart knowledge or to acquire it.
Help us, through this service,
    to appreciate more fully the importance of education –
    in our schools, colleges and universities,
    in adult education and special needs centres,
    in homes and places of work,
    in churches and Sunday schools –
    and, through consecrating all this to you,
    help us to glimpse ways in which each of us,
    however simply,
    might teach or learn ourselves,
    or offer support to those involved in doing so.
In your name we pray.
Amen.

## 173

## Father's Day

### *Romans 8:12-17*

Gracious God,
on this day for remembering, acknowledging
and celebrating fathers,
help us to remember that you call us your children
and that you ask us in turn to call you 'our Father'.
Teach us what that means:
that you care about our welfare;
that you provide for our needs and protect us from danger;
that you delight to bless and cherish;
that you strive to equip us for life,
to teach, guide, support and enable.
Help us, then, as we honour the place of fathers in our lives,
or commit ourselves more fully to faithful parenthood,
also to honour you,
growing and living obediently as your children,
so that we might attain maturity in Christ
and inherit the fullness of life you offer through him.
In his name we pray.
Amen.

## 174

## Harvest

### *Matthew 5:25-34*

Mighty God,
surrounded today by so much
that speaks of your gracious provision,
creative purpose
and sustaining power,
we come now to worship you –
to acknowledge your goodness,
to thank you for your generosity,
to celebrate the wonder of this world
and to rejoice in the rich harvest it so faithfully yields.

Help us again today to recognise how fortunate we are,
    remembering, as we do so, those less fortunate,
    denied their share in the plenty you offer,
    and may that lesson shape our living and loving,
    not just today
    but every day,
    through Jesus Christ our Lord.
Amen.

# 175

## Mothering Sunday

### Mark 10:13-16

Caring and compassionate God,
    speak to us today through the love shown by mothers
    of your love for us and all:
    the love that brought us into being,
    that has nurtured us across the years,
    that welcomes us here
    and that will go on reaching out,
    come what may,
    for all eternity.
Help us, as we honour what motherhood means,
    to honour you also,
    recognising that you show the same devotion and more,
    an unswerving commitment to your children's welfare;
    and teach us, as part of your family,
    to respond accordingly,
    loving you in return,
    expressing our gratitude,
    and living as you have taught us,
    through Jesus Christ our Lord.
Amen.

## 176

## One World Week

*John 3:16*

Lord of all,
    enlarge our vision today and broaden our horizons,
    so that our response to you and to others
    may be enlarged and broadened in turn.
Teach us that we are part not just of the Church
    but also of a wider family of humankind,
    and challenge us to consider what that means,
    what impact it should have on our lives.
Instil in us a willingness to give
    but also to receive,
    to pray for justice
    but also to work for it,
    to see what divides
    but also what unites,
    to stand up for the things we believe in
    but also to respect the convictions of others –
    a readiness, in other words, to recognise
    that this bruised, battered and broken world
    is nonetheless *one* world,
    and, above all, *your* world,
    so precious that you came to it and died for it,
    through Jesus Christ our Lord.
Amen.

## 177

## Prize-giving

*Philippians 3:7-16*

Living God,
    recognising your call to persevere
    in the race you have set before us,
    and to press on towards the prize,
    we come today to acknowledge the young people of this church
    and the efforts they have put in over another year.

Inspire us through the work they have done,
    the targets they have set,
    the lessons learned,
    the fun enjoyed
    and the worship shared.
Help us to appreciate their contribution to our life together,
    and also that of our youth leaders and teachers
    who have given so freely of their time, skill and enthusiasm
    in nurturing young lives among us.
Be with us now, and speak through all we share,
    so that, encouraged by the examples we celebrate,
    we may commit ourselves more fully
    to faithful discipleship in the days ahead,
    through Jesus Christ our Lord.
Amen.

## 178

## Reception of new church member

### *Romans 12:1-21*

Great and wonderful God,
    we thank you for this opportunity to come together,
    at your invitation,
    to share fellowship with you and one another.
We thank you for your gracious call to be your people,
    your children,
    your Church;
    to live and work together as the Body of Christ,
    bearing witness to him through our words and deeds.
Remind us today of the responsibilities that involves
    but also the privilege,
    the challenges it entails
    but also the rewards,
    the expectations it brings of us
    but also the promises it brings from you.
Come now,
    and equip us to honour your call,
    to your glory.
Amen.

# 179

## Rededication service

*Hebrews 6:1-20*

Lord of life
  we would know you better,
  honour you better,
  love you better
  and serve you better.
Meet with us now as we set aside time to worship,
  speak to us as we draw near to listen,
  renew us as we make space to focus on our calling,
  and equip us as we dedicate our lives again to your service.
Through finding you here may we see you everywhere,
  and so live each moment in the light of your love,
  through Jesus Christ our Lord.
Amen.

# 180

## Remembrance Day

*John 15:12-13*

Sovereign God,
  on this day of remembering,
  remind us how much we owe to others
  and how much we owe to you.
Teach us how fortunate we are to enjoy peace,
  how precious a gift that is,
  but speak also of the price
  that securing and maintaining peace can entail;
  the sacrifices so many have made to make it possible,
  the courage they have shown,
  the suffering they have endured
  and the horrors they have seen.
Help us to learn the lessons of the past,
  and also the present,
  honouring all who have served in battle and continue to serve

by doing everything we can
    to promote peace, justice and harmony,
    and also, where necessary, standing up against evil,
    putting the good of others before our own,
    just as you in Christ gave your all.
In his name we pray.
Amen.

## 181

## Songs of Praise / Music

*Ephesians 5:15-20*

Gracious God,
    you call us to sing a new song,
    to make music in our hearts,
    a 'joyful noise to the Lord'.
We come today to do just that:
    to enjoy the gift of music and song,
    not for its own sake alone
    but as an expression of our worship,
    a token of our love,
    a sign of our thankfulness
    and a symbol of our desire to live and work for you,
    lifting up not just our voices
    but also everything we are
    in glad and grateful response.
Bless all we bring you now,
    that it might speak *for* us
    and *to* us,
    in Christ's name.
Amen.

## 182
# Watchnight
### *Revelation 21:5*

Gracious and faithful God,
    on the threshold of another year
    we come to worship you,
    remembering how you have led us over the months gone by
    and anticipating your continued guidance in the days ahead.
We are here to thank you,
    to acknowledge your goodness and love,
    to celebrate the ways you have been with us
    to strengthen, provide, comfort and inspire,
    offering a rock to depend on in all the changing seasons of life.
We are here to praise you,
    confident that whatever the future may hold,
    your grace will be sufficient for all our needs,
    nothing ultimately able to separate us from your love.
We are here, finally,
    to pray for ourselves, our loved ones and our world,
    asking you to bring new beginnings,
    a fresh chapter in which we will come to love and know you better,
    so that we will taste yet more of your goodness
    and be equipped to work more effectively in your service.
Hear us, we pray,
    in the name of Christ.
Amen.

# Time and space for God

## 183

### *Luke 13:31-35*

Gracious God,
  so often we deny ourselves your blessing
  through failing to turn to you;
  failing to respond to your love
  and to receive the mercy, joy, peace and new life
  you so long to bring us.
We come now, therefore,
  making time and space for you,
  and opening our lives to all you would pour into them.
Teach us, as we welcome you today,
  to welcome you equally every day and every moment,
  until you finally welcome us into your eternal kingdom,
  through Jesus Christ our Lord.
Amen.

## 184

### *John 2:1-11*

Lord Jesus Christ,
  remind us afresh today of your transforming power,
  your ability to take something ordinary
  and turn it into something special.
Take, then, our worship,
  and, by your Spirit, make it into something beautiful to you,
  bringing you glory and stirring again our hearts within us.
Take what we are,
  and by your Spirit once more create us anew,
  so that our lives will speak not of our weakness
  but of your saving love and gracious power,
  to the glory of your name.
Amen

# Transforming power of God

## 185

### *John 10:22-30*

Lord Jesus Christ,
  just as your words and actions were one –
  each reinforcing the other, so that everything you said and did
  testified to the loving purpose of your Father in heaven –
  so may our lives likewise speak with one voice,
  bearing eloquent witness to your transforming power
  and redeeming love,
  and to the joy, hope, peace and purpose we have found in you.
Speak to us now,
  so that everything we are may speak for you always,
  to the glory of your name.
Amen.

## 186

### *Mark 1:21-28*

Lord Jesus Christ,
  as crowds in Galilee marvelled at your words and deeds,
  recognising in you an authority
  unlike anything they had seen before,
  speaking powerfully of God's gracious purpose
  and involvement in their lives,
  so, we pray, minister to us now,
  speaking again your redeeming word
  and revealing once more your renewing power.
Open our eyes to your saving grace and healing love,
  to all you are doing in our lives and our world,
  so that the gospel might come alive for us each day,
  ringing true in our daily experience,
  causing us to marvel and rejoice in turn,
  giving thanks for the evidence you provide
  of God's voice speaking afresh
  and his hand at work among us.
Amen.

## 187

*Luke 17:11-19*

Sovereign God,
 speak to us afresh through your word and this time of worship.
Help us, through standing in your presence,
 to make sense of the changes and chances of this life –
 the experiences that puzzle and bewilder,
 the questions that baffle,
 the facts that seem to undermine and even contradict our faith.
Though much may frustrate your purpose and grieve your heart,
 teach us that, through your great love and power,
 you are able to turn sorrow to joy
 and darkness to light,
 somehow bringing good even out of evil.
In that faith may we trust you,
 now and always,
 in Jesus' name.
Amen.

## 188

*John 2:13-22*

Lord Jesus Christ,
 as you cleansed the temple in Jerusalem,
 turning out everything that defiled it,
 that prevented it from fulfilling its true purpose
 and that separated rather than united people with you,
 so come now to our lives and cleanse our hearts,
 removing in turn all that is unworthy,
 that prevents us from being the people you would have us be,
 that destroys our relationship with you.
Re-create us,
 making our bodies into a living temple,
 honouring to you and filled by your presence,
 so that we may truly worship you now
 and faithfully serve you always,
 by your grace.
Amen.

## 189

*John 14:15-21*

Loving God,
 we want to worship you, not just now but always –
 through faithful discipleship and obedience to your will,
 through lives of love pleasing in your sight –
 but we cannot do it by ourselves:
 we need your help.
Draw near through your Spirit of truth,
 and, through the power of the risen Christ,
 transform, re-create and make us new,
 so that we may praise you now and honour you always,
 to the glory of your name.
Amen.

## 190

*John 11:45*

Transforming God,
 turning sorrow to joy,
 doubt to faith,
 despair to hope,
 and death to life,
 put your hand upon us,
 and through this time set apart for you
 continue to make us new.
Turn our weakness into strength,
 our pride into humility,
 our anxiety into trust,
 and our faithlessness into obedience.
Take what we are,
 and, by your resurrection power, shape what we shall be,
 through Jesus Christ our Lord.
Amen.

## 191

*John 2:1-11*

Lord Jesus Christ,
    take the water of our worship and our lives,
    and turn it into wine.
Through your gracious touch,
    transform what we are
    and all we offer
    into something special,
    honouring to you and pleasing in your sight.
Work your miracle within us
    as a sign of the new life you offer to all.
In your name we pray.
Amen.

## 192

*John 2:1-11*

Lord Jesus Christ,
    come among us and, by your grace,
    work your miracle of renewal once more in our hearts.
Where the sparkle has gone out of life,
    where joy is lacking,
    where hope seems exhausted
    or where resources seem to have run dry,
    bring the wine of new life,
    welling up within us
    and bubbling over into spontaneous celebration,
    resurgent faith
    and confidence in your ability to see us through
    to new beginnings.
In your name we ask it.
Amen.

## 193

*Luke 7:11-17*

Almighty God,
  remind us today of your power, strength and authority,
  your ability to create out of nothing
  and to re-create out of the most unlikely materials.
Teach us that nothing is ultimately beyond you;
  that you are constantly fashioning our lives,
  day after day bringing new beginnings and fresh hope,
  new life even out of death.
Help us then, whatever we face,
  and however inadequate
  our resources may seem to meet life's challenges,
  to put our faith in you,
  knowing that you will hear and answer.
Amen.

# Way of Christ

## 194
### *Luke 3:1-6*

Lord Jesus Christ,
    prepare your way in our hearts
    and make us ready to worship you.
Through our praying, thinking, singing and reading
    cleanse our thoughts,
    kindle our faith,
    renew our commitment
    and increase our love,
    preparing your way in our lives,
    so that we might be ready to follow you faithfully
    and serve you more effectively,
    to the glory of your name.
Amen.

## 195
### *Mark 8:27-38*

Redeemer Christ,
    we come to acknowledge you again as our Lord and Saviour;
    to declare our faith in you as the one who sets us free,
    delivering us from all that holds us captive
    and denies us life.
Yet we come also knowing how easily we turn serving you
    into serving self,
    being happy enough to receive
    but reluctant to give,
    ready to profess allegiance when it suits us
    but unwilling to take up our cross should following prove costly.
Equip us, then, through our worship,
    to honour you not just with protestations of loyalty
    but above all with lives committed to your kingdom
    and lived in obedience to your will.
In your name we pray.
Amen.

## 196

### *Mark 13:24-37*

Lord Jesus Christ,
    just as you walked and talked on our earth,
    present among your people,
    sharing our humanity,
    ministering your love,
    living and dying alongside us,
    teach us that you are here now through your Spirit,
    equally as near and involved,
    just as eager to show your love and minister your grace.
Grant, as we come together in your name,
    that we might sense your presence,
    hear your voice
    and learn more of your redeeming, renewing power,
    so that we will be open to all you would do among us
    and equipped to live more faithfully as your people,
    to your glory.
Amen.

## 197

### *John 12:20-33*

Lord Jesus Christ,
    speak to us of the new life you have made possible
    through your stupendous sacrifice,
    your willingness to surrender all.
Unfold to us the true nature of discipleship –
    what it means to love and follow you –
    and help us, by your grace, to respond,
    dying to self and rising to new life with you,
    so that all we do and are may be by your power,
    in your service
    and to your glory.
Amen.

## 198
### *Mark 9:38-50*

Sovereign God,
    we would draw close and learn of you,
    so that we might know, love and serve you better.
Receive, then, the worship we bring
    and meet us through it,
    speaking your word,
    offering your guidance,
    imparting your strength
    and granting your mercy.
Give us a clearer understanding of your will
    and help us to recognise everything in our lives
    that conspires against it;
    that leads us astray,
    separating us from you and one another.
Grant us grace to resist temptation,
    and to walk in your way,
    now and always.
Amen.

## 199
### *Matthew 5:21-37*

Lord Jesus Christ,
    we mean to be faithful to you,
    to live as you have called us to,
    but somehow we repeatedly end up
    turning the positive message of the gospel
    into a list of negatives,
    a matter of rules and regulations rather than grateful response,
    a law that imprisons rather than a love that liberates.
Forgive us,
    and teach us again your way –
    the way of mercy and understanding that leads to life.
In your name we pray.
Amen.

## 200
### *Matthew 13:31-33, 44-52*

Lord Jesus Christ,
   again we ask you to teach us more of your way –
   to open our hearts and minds to your presence among us
   and to your work in our lives and our world.
Help us, today, to understand more clearly
   the nature of your kingdom,
   growing inexorably among us despite all that frustrates your will
   and conspires against your love.
Equip us simply but sincerely to respond to you,
   committing ourselves wholeheartedly to discipleship
   and doing whatever we can in our own small way
   to bring your kingdom closer,
   here on earth as it is in heaven.
Amen.

# Witnessing to Christ

## 201

### Luke 5:1-11

Lord Jesus Christ,
  remind us again today that,
  unworthy though we are,
  you have called us to faith and discipleship,
  to be your witnesses here on earth.
Equip us, then, to honour you,
  for we cannot do so alone,
  there being so little right in us
  and so much wrong.
Speak once more your word of call,
  of mercy
  and of life,
  and send us out to serve you,
  in your strength
  and for your kingdom's sake.
Amen.

## 202

### Mark 4:26-34

Loving God,
  by your grace plant new seeds of faith within us today,
  and through your Spirit feed and nurture them,
  so that, however small that faith might be,
  it may grow and flourish within us
  beyond anything we might imagine.
Grow in our lives,
  that we might sow seeds in the lives of others,
  each of us, through our life and witness,
  insignificant in themselves,
  contributing to the expansion of your kingdom,
  the furthering of your will on earth,
  as it is in heaven.
Amen.

## 203
### *Matthew 28:16-20*

Almighty God,
 we remember today that you are Lord of all,
 not just the few;
 that your purpose embraces the whole world,
 not just the Church.
Help us through this time of worship
 to grasp that truth more clearly
 and to understand its implications for discipleship.
Show us the part you would have us play
 in speaking and working for you,
 showing your love in action
 and witnessing to the new life we have found in you.
Inspire us through the example of others –
 those who, in different ways,
 have responded to your call to make disciples,
 carrying the gospel out to the ends of the earth –
 and equip us, in our own way,
 however small it may seem,
 to honour in turn that highest of callings,
 through Jesus Christ our Lord.
Amen.

# Word of God

## 204
### *Matthew 13:1-9, 18-23*

Living God,
    as we meet together now,
    sow the seed of your word in our hearts.
May it find a place to grow,
    despite all that competes for space in our lives.
May shoots of faith be able to withstand
    the temptations and pressures that threaten to choke them.
May new growth be seen among us,
    leading to a rich harvest of lives won for you.
In Christ's name we ask it.
Amen.

## 205
### *Mark 10:17-31*

Almighty God,
    your word is unsettling, demanding, searching –
    asking of us questions we'd rather not face,
    summoning us to service that seems beyond us,
    examining our innermost thoughts,
    the intentions of the heart,
    and calling for new beginnings,
    radical change –
    yet we need to hear it,
    for we know also that it offers the way to life;
    to peace, joy, hope and fulfilment,
    both now and for all eternity.
So we approach you once more,
    asking you to speak again and to help us listen,
    that we might respond afresh
    to your life-changing yet life-giving voice,
    through Jesus Christ our Lord.
Amen.

## 206

### *Luke 4:14-21*

Lord Jesus Christ,
    as you expounded the Scriptures during your earthly ministry,
    unfolding their true meaning,
    so, we ask, unfold them to us now,
    through your Spirit.
Help us to grasp more clearly the nature of your kingdom,
    the extent of your love,
    and the responsibilities that Christian commitment entails,
    both to you and others.
Save us from closing our ears to that which challenges and disturbs,
    stretching our horizons and questioning comfortable assumptions.
Open our minds and hearts to all you would say to us,
    for your name's sake.
Amen.

## 207

### *John 1:1-18*

Creator God,
    made known to us in the Word made flesh,
    revealing your grace and truth through him
    and bringing light into the darkness of our world,
    come again to us now
    and dwell among us through your Spirit.
Breathe life within us –
    new life born not of the flesh but of you,
    so that your Word might work within us,
    speaking to our hearts,
    illuminating our minds
    and shining from our lives,
    to your glory.
Amen.

# Index of principal themes

# Index of related Bible readings